DR. ENDYA PERRY

GROUNDED AND ROOTED

Firmly planted in the nutrient-rich word of God

Grounded and Rooted: Firmly planted in the nutrient-rich word of God

Unless otherwise noted, Scripture quotations are taken from the Holy Bible, New King James Version.

Library of Congress Cataloging – in – Publication Data

Author: Endya Danielle Perry
Title: Grounded and Rooted: Firmly planted in the nutrient-rich word of God
Registration Number: TXu 2-344-898
Identifiers:
ISBN 979-8-9874746-2-4 (paperback)
ISBN 979-8-9874746-0-0 (hardcover)
ISBN 979-8-9874746-1-7 (e-book)

Acknowledgements

To God, my Creator, Savior, and Lord: This book is a testament of your love and grace. For it was your love and grace that created me for a purpose. It was your love and grace that gave me the strength to survive the valley of the shadow of death. Your love and grace allows me to know the power that lies within the victory of overcoming. Your love and grace empowers me to grow and thrive in you. Therefore I worship you; and I praise you.

This book is a sacrifice of praise to God. God led me on a journey to recognize and fortify my spiritual foundation. At various points in life, I have to revisit the areas covered in this book to strengthen the foundational nutrients I need to continue to grow and thrive in Christ.

To my family: I truly value, treasure, and appreciate all the love, support, and encouragement you have given me. You teach, inspire, and edify me, challenging me to be better every day. I am forever grateful for our family's legacy of redefining the word "possible". I am committed to doing my part in extending that legacy further.

To those who will read this book and leverage it to obtain the spiritual growth and development that is meant for them: You are about to embark on a journey of spiritual strengthening. All glory goes to God, who is the Shepherd and Guide on this transformative journey. Let's Get Started!

Table of Contents

Introduction

There is a quotation that states, "they tried to bury us; but they did not know we were seeds." This quotation is a powerful reminder that when we are faced with seemingly overwhelming circumstances, we can choose to have the perspective that I am not buried; I am planted. As long as we are planted in healthy soil, soil that contains nutrients that will help us to grow, then our planting season breeds anticipation. For we know that the nutrients within the soil serve a purpose that will result in growth and in fruit.

When I reflect on my spiritual journey, I am so thankful to know that I am grounded and rooted in soil that contains rich nutrients. These nutrients have built a strong root system, and a strong foundation, from which I am able to grow. This soil, and the nutrients within the soil, have served a great purpose for me throughout my journey. My journey has had its share of valleys. My journey has had its share of challenges and difficulties. My journey has had its share of brokenness and pain. But a broken tree with strong roots can survive and thrive.

I am therefore at a point in my life where I can stand in a state of thankfulness for my trials, situations, and the various layers of soil I have had to grow through. The nutrients I gathered from those experiences, have created a steadfast strength within me. The word of God has given me the necessary frame, focus, and context as I have traveled through my life journey, thus far. It is the word of God that has enabled me to see the nutrients that are necessary for sustainable spiritual growth.

One essential nutrient in the soil in which we must be rooted is identity. We were created in the image of God. Therefore, it is essential to reveal and to affirm who God truly is; so that in those moments where we may be unsure of our own identity, we can remind ourselves of the image in which we were created. We can remind ourselves of who we are.

Another nutrient in the soil of our spiritual growth is power. By studying the word of God, we can explore miracles of Jesus and the demonstrations of God's power. Through Christ, we can access this power. This is a critical nutrient during cold, dark, and dry seasons where we can feel weak, burned out, and used up. We still have access to power through this nutrient.

The promises God makes to His people are also an essential nutrient for us to gain. It is important to know what we can expect from God, and what God expects from us.

Another nutrient in the soil is mercy. Through this mercy nutrient we see the importance of repentance, forgiveness, and salvation. The nutrients of mercy and grace go hand in hand; but there is a difference.

It is therefore important that we understand the purpose and power of grace, as well. God's goodness is amplified through His grace. He looks beyond our faults; and God meets our needs and grants us blessing in spite of our wrongdoing.

There is a purpose nutrient which facilitates the discovery of God's will for our lives. Along with this discovery of purpose is the recognition of gifts that God has blessed us with and the ways to use and develop these gifts to glorify God. One of the purposes we all share is found within God's commandment to share the gospel of Jesus Christ with others.

The final nutrient covered in this book is the nutrient of praise and worship. This nutrient comes as a result of truly understanding the love of God that serves as the basis for the nutrient-rich soil in which we are planted.

The nutrient-rich soil, which can be accessed through the word of God, provides all we need to grow and to thrive. God provides the other components needed for growth; He provides us with sunlight and rain. But we have to do our part in getting and remaining grounded and rooted in the word of God. To accomplish this, we must spend time reading, reflecting, studying and applying the lessons found within the Bible to our lives. This book provides a guide to begin or continue the journey and reward of grounding and rooting ourselves in the word of God.

Life is a journey. Each person has their own road to travel. Each person has their own experiences and choices they must make. However, there are certain things that every road has in common. Every road will have mountaintops; and every road will have valleys. Every road will have joys; and every road will have pains. But those that accept Jesus as Lord and Savior do not walk alone. The Bible says in Deuteronomy 31:6, "He will never leave you, nor forsake you." Jesus says in Matthew 28:20, "...And lo, I am with you always, even until the end of the age." Therefore, whether we are on the mountaintop rejoicing, or going through the valley, we are not alone.

We can rest with the assurance that the Lord God Almighty is with us and will provide whatever we may be lacking.

Whether we are lacking joy, peace, humility, forgiveness, grace, or mercy, He is more than able to provide all that we need to successfully complete our journey of life.

Once we accept Jesus as Lord and Savior, it is critically important that we take the necessary steps to grow. We must walk the path of spiritual growth. There is no benefit to getting on the right track and not moving. If I am trying to get to a destination, it is not beneficial for me to get onto the correct interstate and park my car in the middle of the highway. I would get run over or knocked off the road. However, if I get on the right road, and I move forward and progress, I will reach my destination.

The same is true of our spiritual journey. We must realize that there is only one way to the father. Jesus says in John 14, "I am the way, the truth, and the life. No one comes to the

Father except through me." However, we must do more than simply come to this realization. We must move forward in Christ. We must not look back or turn around. We must proclaim as Paul did in Philippians 3:13, "Brethren, I count not myself to have apprehended: but this one thing I do, forgetting those things which are behind, and reaching forth unto those things which are before, I press toward the mark for the prize of the high calling of God in Christ Jesus."

This book will assist the body of Christ in its progression toward the "mark for the prize of the high calling of God in Christ Jesus." God's word is "a lamp unto our feet and a light unto our path." He will lead and guide us on this path of growth through His word. He will show us the way, and if we are willing to follow and obey His word, we will reach our destination. We will achieve Spiritual Growth!

Nutrient 1 – Identity

The Intention of This Nutrient:

There are times when life can hit you so hard that you forget who you are. We are made in the image of God. Therefore, on the salvation journey, we must know who God is as we are looking to Him for salvation, guidance, and direction. Whether you are beginning your spiritual journey, or you are already on the journey, the nutrient of identity is a critical component to strength and growth. It is critical to gain and sustain an understanding of who God is and of who we are in Him.

At some carnivals and events, they have an attraction called a funhouse mirror. In this attraction, you would walk into a space full of mirrors. Parts of these mirrors are curved or tilted, which creates a distorted reflection. Therefore, when you look at the mirrors, the mirrors reflect a distorted view of yourself. Some of these mirrors may make you seem far too tall or far too short. Some may make you seem much wider or much thinner than you are. There are situations in life that occur where we can find ourselves in spaces or circumstances that cause us to see a distortion of who we truly are. We can know that we are more than a conqueror. But we can have a defeated thought that turns into a defeated belief and emotion. We can know that we are forgiven and that we have mercy. But we can go through a season where the reflection we see in our actions and behaviors are riddled with guilt and shame.

This nutrient is intended to establish our understanding of who we serve. By increasing our knowledge of who we serve, we will understand the image in which we were created. We will know who has our back. As the Bible says, "if God be for you, then who can be against you."

Identity

1 John 5:7 states, "For there are three that bear witness in heaven: the Father, the Word, and the Holy Spirit; and these three are one." This scripture is referring to the trinity-God, the father; Jesus, the Son (the Word); and the Holy Spirit. John 1:1 states, "In the beginning was the Word, and the Word was with God, and the Word was God. He was in the beginning with God. All things were made through Him, and without Him nothing was made that was made." John 1:14 makes it clear that Jesus is the "Word". It says, "The Word became flesh and made His dwelling among us. We have seen His glory, the glory of the One and Only, who came from the Father, full of

grace and truth." God and Jesus were there from the beginning. When man sinned in the Garden of Eden, he was to be separated from God forever. However, being the merciful God that He is, He sent His only begotten son into the sin-filled Earth to offer the perfect sacrifice so that we might be reconciled to Him. After Jesus died on the cross and rose again, there was a need for man to be able to exemplify the same power and the same assurance that Jesus possessed. Therefore, Jesus said in John 14, "But the Comforter, which is the Holy Spirit, whom the Father will send in my name. He shall teach you all things, and bring all things to your remembrance, whatsoever I have said unto you." Acts 1:8 states, "But ye shall receive power, after that the Holy Spirit is come upon you: and ye shall be witnesses unto me both in Jerusalem, and in all Judea, and in Samaria, and unto the uttermost part of the Earth."

I Am Who I Am

Foundational Scripture

Exodus 3: 1-14. Now Moses was
tending the flock of Jethro his father-
in-law, the priest of Midian. And he
led the flock to the back of the desert,
and came to Horeb, the mountain of
God. 2 And the Angel of
the LORD appeared to him in a flame
of fire from the midst of a bush. So,
he looked, and behold, the bush was
burning with fire, but the
bush was not consumed. 3 Then Moses
said, "I will now turn aside and see
this great sight, why the bush does not
burn." 4 So when the LORD saw that
he turned aside to look, God called to
him from the midst of the bush and
said, "Moses, Moses!" And he said,
"Here I am." 5 Then He said, "Do not
draw near this place. Take your
sandals off your feet, for the place
where you stand is holy
ground." 6 Moreover He

said, "I am the God of your father—
the God of Abraham, the God of
Isaac, and the God of Jacob." And
Moses hid his face, for he was afraid
to look upon God. 7 And
the LORD said: "I have surely seen the
oppression of My people who are in
Egypt, and have heard their
cry because of their taskmasters, for I
know their sorrows. 8 So I have come
down to deliver them out of the hand
of the Egyptians, and to bring them up
from that land to a good and large
land, to a land flowing with milk and
honey, to the place of the Canaanites
and the Hittites and the Amorites and
the Perizzites and the Hivites and the
Jebusites. 9 Now therefore, behold, the
cry of the children of Israel has come
to Me, and I have also seen
the oppression with which the
Egyptians oppress them. 10 Come
now, therefore, and I will send you to
Pharaoh that you may bring My
people, the children of Israel, out of
Egypt." 11 But Moses said to

God, "Who am I that I should go to
Pharaoh, and that I should bring the
children of Israel out of Egypt?" 12 So
He said, "I will certainly be with you.
And this shall be a sign to you that I
have sent you: When you have
brought the people out of Egypt, you
shall serve God on this mountain."
13 Then Moses said to God,
"Indeed, when I come to the children
of Israel and say to them, 'The God of
your fathers has sent me to you,' and
they say to me, 'What is His name?'
what shall I say to them?" 14 And God
said to Moses, "I AM WHO I AM."
And He said, "Thus you shall say to
the children of Israel, 'I AM has sent
me to you.'"

There are many descriptions in the Bible of who God is. In Exodus 3, God appears to Moses and commissions him to deliver the people from slavery in Egypt. In verse 13 Moses asks God, "who shall I say sent me?" In verse 14

God replied, "I am who I am." And He said, "Thus you shall say to the children of Israel, I am has sent me to you." In this one simple phrase God expresses His permanence. God does not change.

God knew that Moses was going to face Pharaoh, a king who expects all who come in contact with him to bow down and serve him. Pharaoh was used to people compromising and falling in line with his commands. However, God stated, "I am who I am." There is no compromise. Once God speaks a word, He is faithful to perform it. Despite adversity, He is God. On the mountaintop, He is God. In the valley, He is God. In times of chaos, He is God. In times of peace, He is God. Early in the morning, He is God. Late in the midnight hour, He is God. He is who He is.

We must also be consistent. Come what may, we must be children of God.

We must take the stand, "I am who I am. Though you may talk about me, I am who I am. Though you may mistreat me, I am who I am. Though you may lie on me, I am who I am. Though everyone else might go in a different direction, I am who I am. Regardless of the situation or circumstance, I AM WHO I AM! I am like a tree that is planted by the water. I shall not be moved. For I have a God who is a sustainer. I have a God that will hold my hand. I have a God that will help me to stand. My God does not change. He is who he is! So, despite what I may go through: despite what I may face, I can "hold to God's unchanging hand."

His Name Shall Be Called

Foundational Scripture

Isaiah 9:2-6. The people who walked in darkness Have seen a great light; Those who dwelt in the land of the

shadow of death, upon them a light
has shined. 3 You have multiplied the
nation and increased its joy; They
rejoice before You According to the
joy of harvest, as men rejoice when
they divide the spoil. 4 For You have
broken the yoke of his burden and the
staff of his shoulder, The rod of his
oppressor, as in the day of Midian.
5 For every warrior's sandal from the
noisy battle, and garments rolled in
blood, Will be used for
burning and fuel of fire. 6 For unto us
a Child is born, unto us a Son is
given; And the government will be
upon His shoulder. And His name will
be called Wonderful,
Counselor, Mighty God, Everlasting
Father, Prince of Peace.

Isaiah 9:2-6 is another scripture passage that identifies who God is. This scripture is mainly speaking of the birth of Jesus Christ. However, as stated in John 1:1, Jesus was there in the beginning of time. Before He was made into flesh, He existed in the heavenly realm.

He is the Light (verse 2) - In Isaiah 9:2 the Bible refers to Jesus as a light. When in sin, we are in a world of darkness. We do not see clearly. We are lost. Isaiah 59:9 speaks of this sinful state. It states, "Therefore justice is far from us; we look for light but there is darkness; for brightness, but we walk in blackness." But God is a merciful God. In Isaiah 60:1-3, it states, "Arise, shine for the light is come! And the glory of the Lord is risen upon you. For behold the darkness shall cover the Earth and deep darkness the people; but the Lord will arise over you and His glory will be seen upon you. The Gentiles shall come to your light, and kings to the brightness of your rising." Jesus is our light. For His word is a "lamp unto our feet and a light unto our path." John 1:4-5 states, "In Him was life and the life was the light of men. And the light shines in the darkness and the darkness did not comprehend it." Jesus is an everlasting light. Nothing can overshadow the light of God; and nothing can dim the light of God. Either we live in darkness, or we walk in the light. Either we remain lost in an unclear world, or we look to Jesus who is the ONE way, truth, and life.

He is a Deliverer (verse 4) - Isaiah 9:4 speaks of God's role as a deliverer. In 2 Chronicles 20, Jehoshaphat was facing a battle with the Moabites, Ammonites, and others. It seemed they would be outpowered. But at the onset of this war, after realizing what he was about to face, Jehoshaphat did not gather his weapons. He did not seek his secretary of war and defense. He did not begin drafting a plan of attack. But verse 3 states that Jehoshaphat proclaimed a fast. He sought God for help. He looked unto the hills from which cometh his help. He sought council in the wise and all-knowing

God. He knew that with his army alone, he did not have a chance against the vast armies and forces he was facing. But he relied on the power of God. He gave up control. And in verse 14 the spirit of God fell upon Jehezial; and in verse 15 he states, "Do not be afraid or discouraged because of this vast army. For the battle is not yours, but God's." And in verse 17 God speaks through Jehezial again and states, "You will not have to fight this battle. Take up your positions; stand firm and see the deliverance the Lord will give you, O Judah and Jerusalem. Do not be afraid; do not be discouraged. Go out to face them tomorrow, and the Lord will be with you." God is a deliverer. Whatever problem or situation you may face. If you give up your false sense of control and allow God to demonstrate His power, He will deliver. He will set free. His will shall be done.

Call His Name - In verse 6 the

scripture goes into further detail of the role of Jesus. The latter part of the verse states, "And His name shall be called..." We must call on His name. Psalms 91:14-15 states, "Because he has set his love upon me, therefore I will deliver him. I will set him on high, because he has known my name. He shall call upon me, and I will answer him; I will be with him in trouble; I will deliver him and honor him." In Matthew 9:27-31 the Bible speaks of two blind men that called to Jesus saying, "Jesus, son of David, have mercy on us." Jesus healed them. We cannot rely on earthly people or possessions to satisfy our needs. We must call on the name of Jesus. For Paul tells us in Philippians 2:10, that "at the name of Jesus every knee shall bow, and every tongue shall confess that Jesus is Lord of all."

His name shall be called Wonderful – God is full of wonder! He is indeed a wonderful savior. Psalms 139:14

states, "I will praise you, for I am fearfully and wonderfully made; Marvelous are your works, and that my soul knows very well." From the sun to the moon, to the trees, to you and me; His works and creations are wonderful. He is an awesome God. His peace is wonderful. His love is wonderful. His power is wonderful. He gave His life for sinners like you and me. He endured the persecution and shame of the cross on our behalf. And He still loves us. He is amazing, full of wonder, full of mercy and of grace. He chooses to bless us in spite of our wrongdoing. He chooses to protect us in spite of our lack of willingness to serve. He chooses to love us in spite of our lack of dedication. He is able to look beyond our faults and see our needs. He is truly wonderful.

His name shall be called Counselor - In Matthew 11:28 He says, "Come to me all you who labor and are heavy laden and I will give you rest." He takes us just as we are, and He molds and mends us. He makes us whole. For truly, I came to Jesus just as I was, weary, wounded and sad. I found in Him a resting place, and He has made me glad. Is there a better counsel than one whose love can never be matched? Is there a greater counsel than one who is all-knowing, all-powerful, and ever-present? God does not have hectic office hours. He neither slumbers nor sleeps. He has our best interests at heart for He created us in his image. What a wonderful counselor we have.

His name shall be called Mighty God - Psalms 24:8 states, "Who is the King of Glory? The Lord strong and mighty, the Lord mighty in battle." When God appeared before Abraham to reveal His promise, He first identified Himself. He states in Genesis 17:1, "I am Almighty God." The promises that God was about to make to Abraham were completely out of the scope of any finite mind. God promises a ninety-nine-year-old man with no children that He is going to make him the father of many nations. To the finite mind, this is impossible, perhaps even ridiculous. But, where man's mind is limited, God's mind is not. He is God Almighty. There is nothing that is impossible for God. There is no power greater than the power of God. There is no bondage He cannot break. There is no sickness He cannot heal. There is no heartache that God cannot console. He is a mighty God. His promise was fulfilled, and He proved himself to be God Almighty.

His name shall be called Everlasting Father - Psalms 90:2 states, "Before the mountains were brought forth or ever you had formed the Earth and the world, even from everlasting to everlasting. You are God." Hebrews 13:8 states, "Jesus Christ the same yesterday, today, and forever." He is indeed everlasting. We can hold to His unchanging hand. We can rely on His unchanging power. We can rest in His ever-present comfort. The same power, love, and strength that God demonstrated throughout the Bible is available today, if we simply yield to Him and allow Him to have His way.

His name shall be called Prince of Peace - John 14:27 states, " Peace I leave with you, My peace I give to you; not as the world gives do I give to you." Philippians 4:7 states, "and the peace of God, which surpasses all understanding, will guard your hearts and minds through Christ Jesus." Once you become saved you have the Prince of Peace, in the midst of the storm. While the lightning is flashing, we can have peace. While the thunder is rolling, we can have peace. While the wind is blowing, we can have peace. Trees could be falling; rain could be pouring but in the midst of it all we can have peace. In Mark 4:39, Jesus speaks to the storm and simply says, "Peace be still." The disciples looked at each other and asked, "what kind of man is this that the winds and the sea obey Him?" No matter how bad the storm may seem, no matter how long the storm may seem to last, rest assured that all it takes is for God to speak to the storm in your life and say, "Peace, be still."

And His name shall be called Wonderful, Counselor, Mighty God, Everlasting Father, Prince of Peace.

We serve an almighty and all-powerful God. His names reflect his power. When we look at names in general, a name is a word or set of words by which someone or something is known, and to which they respond.

In Matthew 7 Jesus says, "Not everyone who says to Me, 'Lord, Lord,' shall enter the kingdom of heaven, but he who does the will of

My Father in heaven." Jesus is saying that although many people may say Lord, Lord; they don't really know me as Lord. For those that know me as Lord will follow me and do the will of God. As Jesus says in John 10:27 "My sheep hear my voice, and I know them, and they follow me."

When we look at this definition of a name, as it relates to God, we can first focus on the set of words by which we know God, Jesus, and the Holy Spirit.

Who do you say that He is?

Foundational Scripture

Matthew 16:13-19. When Jesus came
into the region of Caesarea Philippi,
He asked His disciples, saying, "Who
do men say that I, the Son of Man,
am?" 14 So they said, "Some say John
the Baptist, some Elijah, and others
Jeremiah or one of the prophets."
15 He said to them, "But who do you

say that I am?" [16] Simon Peter
answered and said, "You are the
Christ, the Son of the living God."
[17] Jesus answered and said to
him, "Blessed are you, Simon Bar-
Jonah, for flesh and blood has not
revealed this to you, but My Father
who is in heaven. [18] And I also say to
you that you are Peter, and on this
rock, I will build My church, and the
gates of Hades shall not prevail
against it. [19] And I will give you the
keys of the kingdom of heaven, and
whatever you bind on Earth will be
bound in heaven, and whatever you
loose on Earth will be loosed in
heaven."

In Matthew 16, Jesus asked his disciples, "Who do men say that I am?" The disciples answered and said, "Some say John the Baptist, some Elijah, and others Jeremiah or one of the prophets." Then Jesus made it more personal and asked them, "But who do you say that I am?" Regardless of what everyone else was saying, Jesus wanted to know what those closest to Him believed. Simon Peter answered and said, "You are the Christ, the Son of the living God."

Jesus responds and says that Simon Peter is blessed and says that He will build His church on this rock. The rock Jesus was referring to was Simon Peter's belief and strength in the knowledge of Jesus' identity. Once we have this belief, the scripture says that the gates of Hell cannot prevail against it. We will then have the keys to the kingdom for we know how to access the riches of heaven. For we will have the strength in knowing everything we need is obtained through Jesus. Jesus then also states that whatever we bind on Earth will be bound in heaven; and whatever we loose on Earth would be loosed in heaven. The key to it all is Jesus.

Peter was able to respond because he knew who Jesus was to him.

Even today, we hear people try to classify Jesus or minimize Him. Some people still say He was only a prophet or only a man who once lived. They may call Him those things. But they cannot make me doubt Him, because I know too much about Him. I can call Him my savior because He saved me from my sin. I can call Him my redeemer because He redeemed me. I can call Him Jehovah Jireh, my provider, because He provided for me when I did not have a way to provide for myself. He does not just provide for me in the financial area, He provides me with information, ideas, and joy when I need it. I can call him Jehovah Rapha, my healer, because He has healed my body. I can call Him Jehovah Shalom, because He is my peace.

As the definition suggests it is not just how we know Him, but it is also what He responds to. If we are talking about God responding, we must first talk about faith. Faith activates the power; faith makes a difference. Going back to Matthew 7, when Jesus said that not everyone who calls Him "Lord, Lord, will enter the Kingdom of God," it is faith that makes the difference. When you truly know Him as Lord, you will have the faith to say where you lead me, Lord I will follow. When you call Him and believe in the power of His name and in the power of who He is, you will activate that power, mountains will move, storms will cease, and you will be saved. Paul tells us in Romans 10, that "whoever calls on the name of the Lord shall be saved."

The Name of Jesus

Foundational Scripture

Acts 3:1-10. Now Peter and John

went up together to the temple at the
hour of prayer, the ninth hour. 2 And a
certain man lame from his mother's
womb was carried, whom they laid
daily at the gate of the temple which
is called Beautiful, to ask alms from
those who entered the temple; 3 who,
seeing Peter and John about to go into
the temple, asked for alms. 4 And
fixing his eyes on him, with John,
Peter said, "Look at us." 5 So he gave
them his attention, expecting to
receive something from them. 6 Then
Peter said, "Silver and gold I do not
have, but what I do have I give
you: In the name of Jesus Christ of
Nazareth, rise up and walk." 7 And he
took him by the right hand and
lifted him up, and immediately his
feet and ankle bones received
strength. 8 So he, leaping up, stood
and walked and entered the temple
with them—walking, leaping, and
praising God. 9 And all the people saw
him walking and praising
God. 10 Then they knew that it was he

who sat begging alms at the Beautiful
Gate of the temple; and they were
filled with wonder and amazement at
what had happened to him.

Acts 4:1-12. Now as they spoke to the
people, the priests, the captain of the
temple, and the Sadducees came upon
them, [2] being greatly disturbed that
they taught the people and preached
in Jesus the resurrection from the
dead. [3] And they laid hands on them,
and put them in custody until the next
day, for it was already
evening. [4] However, many of those
who heard the word believed; and the
number of the men came to be about
five thousand. [5] And it came to pass,
on the next day, that their rulers,
elders, and scribes, [6] as well as Annas
the high priest, Caiaphas, John, and
Alexander, and as many as were of
the family of the high priest, were
gathered together at Jerusalem. [7] And
when they had set them in the midst,
they asked, "By what power or by

what name have you done this?"
[8] Then Peter, filled with the Holy
Spirit, said to them, "Rulers of the
people and elders of Israel: [9] If we this
day are judged for a good
deed done to a helpless man, by what
means he has been made well, [10] let it
be known to you all, and to all the
people of Israel, that by the name of
Jesus Christ of Nazareth, whom you
crucified, whom God raised from the
dead, by Him this man stands here
before you whole. [11] This is the 'stone
which was rejected by you builders,
which has become the chief
cornerstone.' [12] Nor is there salvation
in any other, for there is no other
name under heaven given among men
by which we must be saved.

Acts 3-4 also expresses what the name of the Lord can do. In Acts 3, Peter and John were going to the temple at the hour of prayer. There was a man that was at the temple gate, who had been paralyzed since his birth. He was carried there to the gate of the temple every day to beg those who were going into the temple courts.

Perhaps some of us can not relate to being paralyzed since birth. But many of us may know what it feels like to be stuck and unable to move out of a situation. Many of us may understand the pain that comes from being placed wherever people choose to place you. Not to mention that the place people choose to place you is often outside of the place where healing, blessing, and joy reside. Others are able to go passed you into the place of blessing and favor. You want the blessing and favor, but you are too broken to get it. You are left outside to beg and ask for help and your voice may often be ignored. This is the state this man was in.

When he saw Peter and John, he begged them for money. Peter said to him "Look at us!" So, the man looked up expecting to get paid. But Peter then said, "Silver or gold I do not have, but what I do have I give you. In the name of Jesus, walk." The man was asking for money, but the man did not need the money as badly as he needed to be healed.

Sometimes we ask for a fix of the visible problem, but the actual wound is much deeper. When we encounter those who are paralyzed in life, or who are broken; or if we are the ones who are broken or feel stuck, we can call on the name of Jesus. For in the name of Jesus is the power to heal, the power to deliver, and the power to save. We may not have the money, we may not have the energy, we may not have the knowledge, but what we do have is the all-powerful and almighty name of Jesus.

In Acts 4, after healing the lame man that was outside the temple, Peter and

John preached the word and about 5,000 people were saved. The Sadducees and leaders of the temple were upset and had Peter and John arrested. The next day Peter and John were brought before the Sadducees and leaders; and they asked them about how they healed the lame man. They said to them, “by what power or by what name did you do this”. Peter responded to say, “It is by the name of Jesus, whom you crucified but whom God raised from the dead, it is by His name that this lame man stands before you healed.” Peter went on to say that “Salvation is found in no one else, for there is no other name under heaven given to man by which we must be saved.”

In addition to this account which demonstrates the power in the name Jesus, I also have another witness for you that can attest to how Jesus will respond when you call on His name – A man named Bartimaeus.

Jesus Responds When We Call

Foundational Scripture

Mark 10: 46-52. Now they came to
Jericho. As He went out of Jericho
with His disciples and a great
multitude, blind Bartimaeus, the son
of Timaeus, sat by the road
begging. [47] And when he heard that it
was Jesus of Nazareth, he began to
cry out and say, "Jesus, Son of
David, have mercy on me!" [48] Then
many warned him to be quiet; but he
cried out all the more, "Son of David,
have mercy on me!" [49] So Jesus stood
still and commanded him to be called.
Then they called the blind man,
saying to him, "Be of good cheer.
Rise, He is calling you." [50] And
throwing aside his garment, he rose
and came to Jesus. [51] So Jesus
answered and said to him, "What do
you want Me to do for you?" The
blind man said to Him, "Rabboni, that
I may receive my sight." [52] Then Jesus

said to him, "Go your way; your faith has made you well." And immediately he received his sight and followed Jesus on the road.

In Mark 10, Jesus and His disciples were in Jericho. As they were leaving the city, there was a blind man named Bartimaeus that was sitting by the roadside. He heard that Jesus was coming through. He began to cry out, "Jesus, Son of David, have mercy on me!" There were many people who told him to be quiet. But the more they tried to silence him, the louder he got "Jesus, Son of David, have mercy on me!" Jesus had Bartimaeus brought to Him, and Jesus asked him, "what do you want me to do for you?" Bartimaeus responded and said, "Lord I want to see." Jesus told him, "Your faith has healed you." Bartimaeus' healing began with him crying out in faith and calling on the name, Jesus.

There is power in the name of Jesus. Do not let anyone stop you from crying out to Jesus. Call on Him. It does not matter what you are up against or what you may be facing, call on the name of Jesus. Because as Paul tells us in Philippians 2, "God has highly exalted Him and given Him the name, which is above every name, that at the name of Jesus every knee shall bow, and every tongue shall confess that He is Lord."

If you are facing problems that seem too big and too much to bear, call on Him because those problems will have to bow down. If you are hearing the voices, even if it is your own voice, that doubt you and try to deny you from that which God is leading you into, call on Him. Those voices will be silenced, as every tongue will confess that He is Lord. And if God is for you then who can be against you?

We are victorious! We are more than conquerors through Christ.

So, we will walk in victory knowing that we have God on our side. We have Jehovah Jireh on our side - God provides for us. We have Jehovah Rapha on our side - God heals us. We have Jehovah Shalom on our side - God is our peace.

Thank you, God, for who you are.

Who Am I?

It is important to know who you are and the power you possess. Because this world has systems specifically designed to deceive you into believing you are less than who you are. There are deliberate institutions created to lead you to believe you have no hope and no power. But we are going to tear down and destroy the deception created by these systems and institution. This world may tell you that you are a lost generation. But the word of God says in 1 Peter 2:9 that "you are a chosen generation, a royal priesthood, a holy nation, a peculiar people, that you may declare the praises of Him who called you out of darkness into his wonderful light." This world may tell you that your life does not matter. But the word of God says in Ephesians 1:11 "In Him we were chosen having been predestined according to the plan of Him who works out everything with the purpose of His will." God says in Jeremiah 29:11 "I know the plans I have for you. Plans for good and not for evil to give you a future and a hope." Romans 12:6 says that each of us have different gifts according to the grace given to us. You matter to God. Your life matters. You have a purpose. You have a future. You have gifts and talents you are called to use. You are chosen. You are God's child.

It is time to silence all the voices that try to speak negativity in your life and replace those voices with God's voice. God is your creator. Therefore, he is the one that knows who you are.

Let's say I invent a new kitchen appliance that does amazing things. With this new appliance, all you have to do is say what you want. This appliance will then gather the ingredients and prepare the meal for you to perfection. But it does not stop there. This appliance plates the meal and delivers it to you, right where you sit. This is an amazing invention!

But let's say you took this appliance outside, and you tried to use it as a car. You would think that this invention is horrible. It does not have wheels. It does not have any mechanism for steering. It does not have any mechanism of ignition or acceleration. You may call it useless. You may call it a waste. But until you ask the creator what its purpose is, you will not know how to get the best out of it. You will not know what it is designed to do. You will miss out on the beauty, power, blessing, and gift that it is.

If you are hearing people speak negativity to you, telling you that you are not good enough, smart enough, resourceful enough, it is likely because they do not know what you are created to do. When you are operating in your purpose for which God has called you, you will see, feel, and know that this is your calling. Do not allow others to label you when they do not know your purpose and calling. Do not allow others to limit you based on where you are today without a knowledge of your journey.

With these things in mind, the only one that can tell you who you are is God; and He loves you. He has a purpose for your life. If you want to know who you are, ask God, who is your creator. Unpack your life's journey that you have lived thus far. Look at your full journey, the darkest and lowest of valleys included, and reveal the themes you see if your life. What are the things within you that have allowed you to come through what you have come through and still be standing? What is it about you that enables you to stand in the middle of the storm that you may be facing right now? What is it that your journey says about you that caused you to reach out to purchase this book to say I know the importance of my foundation and I want to ensure I know the nutrients I need to be firmly grounded and rooted and to know I can stand firm and face whatever may come?

Dismiss the Negativity

Foundational Scripture
Mark 5: 35-43. While He was still
speaking, some came from the ruler of
the synagogue's house who said,
"Your daughter is dead. Why trouble
the Teacher any further?" 36 As soon

as Jesus heard the word that was
spoken, He said to the ruler of the
synagogue, "Do not be afraid;
only believe." [37] And He permitted no
one to follow Him except Peter,
James, and John the brother of
James. [38] Then He came to the house
of the ruler of the synagogue and
saw a tumult and those who wept and
wailed loudly. [39] When He came in,
He said to them, "Why make this
commotion and weep? The child is
not dead, but sleeping." [40] And they
ridiculed Him. But when He had put
them all outside, He took the father
and the mother of the child, and
those who were with Him, and
entered where the child was
lying. [41] Then He took the child by the
hand, and said to her, "Talitha,
cumi," which is translated, "Little
girl, I say to you,
arise." [42] Immediately the girl arose
and walked, for she was twelve
years of age. And they were overcome
with great amazement. [43] But He

commanded them strictly that no one should know it, and said
that something should be given her to eat.

We have to dismiss the negativity and only abide in truth. It is once we dismiss the negative voices and thoughts that God will truly do miraculous things in our world. This aligns with the event captured in Mark 5 when Jairus, one of the rulers of the synagogue, learned that his daughter was gravely ill; so, he came to Jesus for help. Jesus agreed to go to Jairus' house. On the way to his house Jairus received word that his daughter had died. Jesus said to Jairus do not be afraid, just believe. When Jesus arrived at Jairus' house everyone was grieving and crying, wailing due to the pain they felt as this young twelve-year-old girl had passed away. But when Jesus came in the house, he said to them "she's not dead, she is just asleep." When the people there heard what Jesus said, they laughed at Him. They made fun of Him.

Have you ever shared your dreams, your goals, or your calling with someone and they laughed at you? They may have doubted you and told you it will never happen. They may have said you are not good enough; it cannot be done. Well in Mark 5, Jesus revealed to us how to deal with those doubters and haters.

Jesus was well aware of what was going on in the natural realm. But He was speaking of things they could not see in the natural realm. They did not realize that Jesus was in the room; and once Jesus is in the room, the impossible becomes possible. Miracles will happen. Things will turn around. Things that may appear final can be revived. That which was lost can be found. Jesus is in the room. When Jesus came in, he told all those that were laughing and mocking him to get out. Once He got them out, a miracle happened, and the girl rose from the dead.

Let Jesus in the room. Let him fill your heart, your mind, and your life. Let him fill it so that there is no room for negativity. When people speak negatively to you, respond with the word of God. When negative thoughts enter your mind, replace them with the thoughts of God. When people try to tell you what you cannot do, declare as Paul said, "I can do all things through Christ who strengthens me." When you feel tempted to do wrong, declare as stated in James 4:7, "Submit yourself to God, resist the devil and he will flee from you." When people try to make you feel guilty, recall that God says in Isaiah 43:25 "I, even I, am He that blots out your transgressions for My own sake; And I will not remember your sins." Silence those negative voices and thoughts by filling your heart and mind with the word of God.

Be identified by who God says you are. We are new creatures in Christ. We are the head and not the tail. We are more than conquerors through Him who loved us. We are forgiven. We are redeemed. We are greatly loved. Instead of walking around saying what a mighty trial I am going through; we should say "oh what a mighty God I serve." Change the way you talk. Change the way you walk. Change your perspective and change your life. Your bank account balance may be the same, the issues on your job may still be there. But your change in focus will change the way you live. Attach God to your identity and release your insecurities for He will fill every gap you may have. Where you are weak, his strength will prevail. Isaiah says He gives power to the weak and to those who have no might he increases strength.

Just as Jesus had to clear the room, we

have to do the same. We can speak to those negative things that try to cause us to see ourselves as less than we are. Low self-esteem - get out of here! You have no place here. Peer pressure - remove yourself! There is no room for you here. Insecurity and doubt - get out! You have no right to be here. Jesus is in the room. Jesus is in my heart, my thoughts, and my soul. I know who God created me to be. I know who I am.

Nutrient 2 - Power

The Intention of This Nutrient:

At certain points in life we may experience a spiritual power surge. A power surge is defined as an unexpected spike in electrical power running through the electrical system. When we face situations of trauma, pain, confusion, and disaster we often have to employ a significant amount of faith, perseverance, resilience, and strength to survive the situation and season.

In the natural realm, we often recognize a power surge when we need a light or an electrical appliance; and we realize it will not turn on. Similarly, in the spiritual, we may go to reach for our faith or reach for our joy and realize it will not turn on. We can find that the surge from our last storm has resulted in a loss of power. But we have a generator. We do not have to go without power. We have an unlimited power source that we can tap into. For the omnipotent God is our source. We have to regularly check to ensure we understand and are accessing the power God has given us to fulfill our purpose. This understanding and access is part of our wiring and will ensure we do not have a power surge due to faulty wiring.

This nutrient of power provides the assurance that with God all things are possible. The nutrient gives visibility into the expansive nature of God's power. God's power is not limited to one thing or confined to one area of life. God uses His power to fulfill His will. The use of His power aligns with His identity.

Power

God is omnipotent, which means He has unlimited power. God uses His power to create, multiply, heal, protect, guide, and resurrect. By examining what God does with His power, it should lead us to reflect on what we are doing with the impact and influence that we have.

In Matthew 11 John the Baptist was in prison, and he heard of Jesus' miracles and teachings. John then sent his followers to ask Jesus if He was the Messiah. Jesus told John's followers to report what they had seen. Jesus' life work and daily walk demonstrates who He is. What does your life work say about you? Does your life show that you love your neighbors? Does your life show that you have no other gods before the one true God? We should ensure that our lives show that we are children of God. Through your life are you creating, multiplying, healing, protecting, guiding, and resurrecting through the power of God? If your life does not reflect these Christlike characteristics, pray and ask God to help you to live life more abundantly.

The Power to Create

Foundational Scripture

Genesis 1:1-31. In the beginning God
created the heavens and the
Earth. 2 The Earth was without form,
and void; and darkness was on the
face of the deep. And the Spirit of
God was hovering over the face of the
waters. 3 Then God said, "Let there
be light"; and there was light. 4 And
God saw the light, that it was good;
and God divided the light from the
darkness. 5 God called the light Day,
and the darkness He called Night. So,
the evening and the morning were the
first day. 6 Then God said, "Let there
be a firmament in the midst of the

waters, and let it divide the waters
from the waters." [7] Thus God made
the firmament and divided the waters
which were under the firmament from
the waters which were above the
firmament; and it was so. [8] And God
called the firmament Heaven. So, the
evening and the morning were the
second day. [9] Then God said, "Let the
waters under the heavens be gathered
together into one place, and let the
dry land appear"; and it was so. [10] And
God called the dry land Earth, and the
gathering together of the waters He
called Seas. And God saw that it
was good. [11] Then God said, "Let the
Earth bring forth grass, the
herb that yields seed, and the fruit
tree that yields fruit according to its
kind, whose seed is in itself, on the
Earth"; and it was so. [12] And the Earth
brought forth grass, the
herb that yields seed according to its
kind, and the tree that yields fruit,
whose seed is in itself according to its
kind. And God saw that it

was good. [13] So the evening and the
morning were the third day. [14] Then
God said, "Let there be lights in the
firmament of the heavens to divide
the day from the night; and let them
be for signs and seasons, and for days
and years; [15] and let them be for lights
in the firmament of the heavens to
give light on the Earth"; and it was
so. [16] Then God made two great lights:
the greater light to rule the day, and
the lesser light to rule the night. He
made the stars also. [17] God set them in
the firmament of the heavens to give
light on the Earth, [18] and to rule over
the day and over the night, and to
divide the light from the darkness.
And God saw that it was good. [19] So
the evening and the morning were the
fourth day. [20] Then God said, "Let the
waters abound with an abundance of
living creatures, and let birds fly
above the Earth across the face of
the firmament of the
heavens." [21] So God created great sea
creatures and every living thing that

moves, with which the waters
abounded, according to their kind, and
every winged bird according to its
kind. And God saw that it
was good. 22 And God blessed them,
saying, "Be fruitful and multiply, and
fill the waters in the seas, and let birds
multiply on the Earth." 23 So the
evening and the morning were the
fifth day. 24 Then God said, "Let the
Earth bring forth the living creature
according to its kind: cattle and
creeping thing and beast of the
Earth, each according to its kind"; and
it was so. 25 And God made the beast
of the Earth according to its kind,
cattle according to its kind, and
everything that creeps on the Earth
according to its kind. And God saw
that it was good. 26 Then God
said, "Let Us make man in Our image,
according to Our likeness; let them
have dominion over the fish of the
sea, over the birds of the air, and over
the cattle, over all the Earth and over
every creeping thing that creeps on

the Earth." 27 So God created man in
His own image; in the image of God
He created him; male and female He
created them. 28 Then God blessed
them, and God said to them, "Be
fruitful and multiply; fill the Earth
and subdue it; have dominion over the
fish of the sea, over the birds of the
air, and over every living thing
that moves on the Earth." 29 And God
said, "See, I have given you every
herb that yields seed which is on the
face of all the Earth, and every tree
whose fruit yields seed; to you it shall
be for food. 30 Also, to every beast of
the Earth, to every bird of the air, and
to everything that creeps on the Earth,
in which there is life, I have
given every green herb for food"; and
it was so. 31 Then God saw everything
that He had made, and indeed it
was very good. So, the evening and
the morning were the sixth day.

The Bible opens with identifying God and His power to create. The first verse of the Bible states "In the beginning God created the heavens and the Earth." When God creates, He finishes. He creates things in fullness and completion. Verse 2 mentions that initially the Earth was without form, void, and dark. But God did not leave it there; He completed it. He created light to conquer the darkness. He created form by establishing the waters and separating the land and the sky. He addressed the void by creating vegetation and animals. He then created man in His image and with His hands.

After everything God created, He evaluated it and declared that it was good. But in Genesis 2:18 God states "It is not good that man should be alone." God then put Adam to sleep and took one of his ribs and created Eve from that rib.

God created some things through His word. By saying “Let there be light”, light was created. His word is powerful! His word has the power to create. He created other things by His actions. In the beginning he created the heavens and the Earth. The Bible didn’t say he said anything, He just created it. There are things within our lives that God creates out of nowhere and out of nothing. Then there are things that God created with His hands. He created us with His hands. We are now His hands on Earth; and He can create things through us.

When we serve others, we are allowing God’s creative power to flow through us to create solutions for His children. We can create options and possibilities through the power of God. He created us in His image, so we were created to create, as well. As God spoke to Zerubbabel in Zechariah 4:6, it is “not by might, nor by power, but by my Spirit, says the Lord.” That which we create is not for our glory. For whatever we create was created by the use of God's power at work within and through us.

Jesus Creates Peace in the Storm

Foundational Scripture

Mark 4:35-41. On the same day, when
evening had come, He said to
them, "Let us cross over to the other
side." 36 Now when they had left the
multitude, they took Him along in the
boat as He was. And other little boats
were also with Him. 37 And a great
windstorm arose, and the waves beat
into the boat, so that it was already
filling. 38 But He was in the stern,
asleep on a pillow. And they awoke
Him and said to Him, "Teacher, do
You not care that we are perishing?"
39 Then He arose and rebuked the
wind, and said to the sea, "Peace, be
still!" And the wind ceased and there
was a great calm. 40 But He said to

them, “Why are you so fearful? How is it that you have no faith?” 41 And they feared exceedingly, and said to one another, “Who can this be, that even the wind and the sea obey Him!”

After teaching parables, Jesus went out on a ship with His disciples. A great storm arose, and water began to come into the boat. The disciples became frightened; and Jesus was asleep. The disciples woke him up and asked him, “don't you care if we die out here?” Jesus got up and rebuked the wind and spoke to the sea and said, "Peace, be still." He asked them, "Why are you so fearful? How is it that you have no faith?"

The disciples were fine as long as the sea remained calm. They seemed to have faith when things were smooth. But when the storm arose, they allowed their fear to overshadow their faith. They relied on their finite senses, instead of relying on the infinite power of God. They did not realize whom they had on board. They did not realize that they were sailing with the Master of the sea. They did not realize that the one who was on the ship with them is the one who created the wind, the sea, and the rain.

We must realize the power that we possess when Jesus is the captain of our ship. We must realize that as long as He is on board, we will not be overtaken by any storm. He can create peace where there is no peace. He can create peace through his word. No matter how rough it gets, once Jesus speaks to the storm, it has to obey Him.

The Power to Multiply

Foundational Scripture
Matthew 14:13-21. [13] When Jesus
heard *it,* He departed from there by
boat to a deserted place by Himself.
But when the multitudes heard it, they

followed Him on foot from the
cities. 14 And when Jesus went out, He
saw a great multitude; and He was
moved with compassion for them and
healed their sick. 15 When it was
evening, His disciples came to Him,
saying, "This is a deserted place, and
the hour is already late. Send the
multitudes away, that they may go into
the villages and buy themselves food."
16 But Jesus said to them, "They do not
need to go away. You give them
something to eat." 17 And they said to
Him, "We have here only five loaves
and two fish." 18 He said, "Bring them
here to Me." 19 Then He commanded
the multitudes to sit down on the grass.
And He took the five loaves and the
two fish, and looking up to heaven, He
blessed and broke and gave the loaves
to the disciples; and the disciples gave
to the multitudes. 20 So they all ate and
were filled, and they took up twelve
baskets full of the fragments that
remained. 21 Now those who had eaten
were about five thousand men, besides

women and children.

As Jesus was healing the sick in the city, a multitude of over five thousand people gathered around. The disciples suggested to Jesus that they send the multitude away so they could go get something to eat for themselves. In verse 16 Jesus states, "They do not need to go away. You give them something to eat." The disciples then told Jesus that all they had was two fish and five loaves of bread, which they had obtained from a young boy that was present. Jesus took the fish and bread and multiplied it. They were able to feed the multitude, and they were all full; and they had food left over after everyone was fed.

Jesus is able to take our insufficiencies and make them sufficient. He is able to take what we have and multiply it so that it may be used for His glory. We must be willing to give Him all that we have. When we are in the presence of

God, we must realize that He has all the power to meet our needs regardless of the starting point.

With the crowd in Matthew 14, the starting point was two fish and five loaves of bread. For us it may be no income, or no home, or poor health. Whatever the starting point, God is able to supply our needs, and provide overflow. He will make it enough. Your resources – He will make it enough. Your energy – He will make it enough. Your abilities – He will make it enough. YOU – He has made you enough!

The Power of What God Has Already Given You

Foundational Scripture

1 Kings 17:8-16. Then the word of
the LORD came to him,
saying, [9] "Arise, go to Zarephath,
which belongs to Sidon, and dwell
there. See, I have commanded a

widow there to provide for you." [10] So
he arose and went to Zarephath. And
when he came to the gate of the city,
indeed a widow was there gathering
sticks. And he called to her and said,
"Please bring me a little water in a
cup, that I may drink." [11] And as she
was going to get it, he called to her
and said, "Please bring me a morsel of
bread in your hand." [12] So she said,
"As the LORD your God lives, I do not
have bread, only a handful of flour in
a bin, and a little oil in a jar; and see,
I am gathering a couple of sticks that I
may go in and prepare it for myself
and my son, that we may eat it,
and die." [13] And Elijah said to her,
"Do not fear; go and do as you have
said, but make me a small cake from
it first, and bring it to me; and
afterward make some for yourself and
your son. [14] For thus says the Lord
God of Israel: 'The bin of flour shall
not be used up, nor shall the jar of oil
run dry, until the day the LORD sends
rain on the Earth.'" [15] So she went

away and did according to the word of Elijah; and she and he and her household ate for many days. [16] The bin of flour was not used up, nor did the jar of oil run dry, according to the word of the LORD which He spoke by Elijah.

In 1 Kings 17, the Lord provided food for Elijah. In verse 4 God revealed His plan to Elijah. He states, "You shall drink from the brook, and I have commanded the ravens to feed you there." Once the brook dried up, God gave Elijah his next set of instructions. In verse 9 God instructs him to, "Arise, go to Zarephath, which belongs to Sidon, and dwell there. See, I have commanded a widow there to provide for you."

Elijah followed the instructions of God. He asked the widow for something to drink and for some bread. The widow had just enough flour and oil to make bread for her and her son. She had planned to use the last of the flour to make the bread for her and her son, and then they would die. But Elijah tells her in verse 13-14, "Do not fear; go and do as you have said, but make me a small cake from it first, and bring it to me; and afterward make some for yourself and your son. For thus says the Lord God of Israel: 'The bin of flour shall not be used up, nor shall the jar of oil run dry, until the day the Lord sends rain on the Earth.'"

The widow followed the instructions that were sent by God. She first made Elijah bread; then she made bread for her family. And as always, God kept His word, and the jar of flour was not used up and the oil never ran dry until the rain came again.

She was obedient and showed her willingness to serve. She was willing to sacrifice all that she had. For she knew that God would provide. God provided and multiplied. It was enough for her; and she was able to sell the excess to pay her debts. Through Elijah, God was able to reveal to her the value in what she had. God showed her the vastness of what she already had access to. God has the power to provide exponential increase and growth in what we already have.

The Power to Heal

Foundational Scripture

Mark 5:21-43. Now when Jesus had
crossed over again by boat to the
other side, a great multitude gathered
to Him; and He was by the sea. [22] And
behold, one of the rulers of the
synagogue came, Jairus by name. And
when he saw Him, he fell at His
feet [23] and begged Him earnestly,
saying, "My little daughter lies at the
point of death. Come and lay Your
hands on her, that she may be healed,
and she will live." [24] So Jesus went

with him, and a great multitude
followed Him and thronged Him.
[25] Now a certain woman had a flow of
blood for twelve years, [26] and had
suffered many things from many
physicians. She had spent all that she
had and was no better, but rather grew
worse. [27] When she heard about Jesus,
she came behind Him in the crowd
and touched His garment. [28] For she
said, "If only I may touch His clothes,
I shall be made well." [29] Immediately
the fountain of her blood was dried
up, and she felt in her body that she
was healed of the affliction. [30] And
Jesus, immediately knowing in
Himself that power had gone out of
Him, turned around in the crowd and
said, "Who touched My clothes?"
[31] But His disciples said to Him, "You
see the multitude thronging You, and
You say, 'Who touched Me?'" [32] And
He looked around to see her who had
done this thing. [33] But the
woman, fearing and trembling,
knowing what had happened to her,

came and fell down before Him and told Him the whole truth. [34] And He said to her, "Daughter, your faith has made you well. Go in peace and be healed of your affliction."

While Jesus was on the way to Jairus' house to heal his daughter, there was another miracle that was needed. Jesus is never too busy to acknowledge your faith. A woman who had been suffering from a bleeding issue for twelve years pressed her way through the crowd.

Blood streams from a wound. Alice Walker once said, "healing begins where the wound was made." We can experience various types of wounds in life that result in bleeding. Loss of relationships may result in the bleeding of bitterness or doubt. A wound of abuse may result in the bleeding of insecurity or inferiority. The wound of abandonment may result in the bleeding of depression or emptiness. Oftentimes people seek to heal bleeding issues by various methods. If you do not know the healing power of Jesus, you may seek relief and healing from relationships or substance abuse. But these things cannot stop the bleeding or heal the wound. They only provide a temporary relief; and they often make things worse.

We must make our way to Jesus and give it all to Him. Let Him heal the source of our hurt and pain. We must be open and honest with God. He will heal our mind, body, and spirit. He will set us free.

Although in her culture, this woman was considered "unclean", she still made her way to Jesus. She had a thought "If only I may touch His clothes, I shall be made well." Her bleeding was stopped immediately once she touched the hem of his garment.

There is a song that tells the story about this woman who had this bleeding issue. The song states "I tried all I could. Seems like nothing did me any good. Then I heard Jesus that He was passing by, and I decided to give Him a try." And as we see in the story, once this woman touches the hem of His garment, she was made whole. I can imagine that this had to be shocking for her. For twelve years, she had tried everything she could think of to be healed; nothing worked. But with just one touch of Jesus' garment, she was healed. I am sure she wondered, how is this possible? Then the chorus of the song comes in and provides the answer to this question. The chorus of the song says "Oh, it is Jesus. Oh, it is Jesus. It's Jesus in my soul. For I have touched the hem of His garment, and His blood has made me whole."

If you have been searching for a way to end the suffering, oh it is Jesus. If you are searching for ways to ease the emotional, mental, or spiritual pain, oh it is Jesus. The woman with the issue of blood causes us to ask ourselves, "where is your faith? Whose garment are you reaching for?" Jesus has the power to heal. He is the one we should seek.

Do You Want to Experience Jesus' Power?

Foundational Scripture

John 5:1-9. After this there was a
feast of the Jews, and Jesus went up to
Jerusalem. 2 Now there is in
Jerusalem by the Sheep Gate a pool,
which is called in Hebrew, Bethesda,
having five porches. 3 In these lay a
great multitude of sick people, blind,
lame, paralyzed, waiting for the
moving of the water. 4 For an angel
went down at a certain time into the

pool and stirred up the water; then
whoever stepped in first, after the
stirring of the water, was made well
of whatever disease he had. 5 Now a
certain man was there who had an
infirmity thirty-eight years. 6 When
Jesus saw him lying there, and knew
that he already had been in that
condition a long time, He said to
him, "Do you want to be made well?"
7 The sick man answered Him, "Sir, I
have no man to put me into the pool
when the water is stirred up; but while
I am coming, another steps down
before me." 8 Jesus said to him, "Rise,
take up your bed and walk." 9 And
immediately the man was made well,
took up his bed, and walked. And that
day was the Sabbath.

In this chapter, Jesus arrives at the pool called Bethesda in Jerusalem. At this pool, those with various ailments would gather with the hope that they would be the first to the pool once the water is stirred, so that they would be healed. This was a belief in their custom. When Jesus arrived, He found a man there who had been paralyzed for thirty-eight years.

Thirty-eight years is a long time. When you have been in the same condition for a long time, it can consume and overtake you. You can begin to develop your daily routine and daily demeanor around your condition. As we see in the text, that condition became this man's identity. Verse 5 does not refer to this man by his name. The man is referred to as the man with an infirmity. Your words, actions, and everyday walk is how people will identify you. Instead of calling you by name, you can be referred to as "that woman that's always complaining" or "that man that always has an attitude". Do not get comfortable in negative situations or with negative reactions. Do not get comfortable in chaos. Instead, get comfortable with Christ. Instead of being consumed with your circumstance, get a hold of the all-consuming fire of the Holy Spirit.

When Jesus saw the man lying there, He knew he had been in that condition for a long time. Jesus asked him "Do you want to be made well?" This was a valid question. In that day and in that culture, the many people who had ailments that gathered there knew they all would not be healed. But they often used this forum to beg for money and goods. This was a lucrative profession for them. So, there were some that would prefer to stay in this state to receive money and items in this manner, instead of being healed and having to work for it. This is the reason Jesus asked the question.

People can get accustomed to the attention they receive when they are in a condition they can talk about. For some people they feel the only time they receive a kind word, or a hug, or a prayer is to succumb to a depressing situation. As people of God, we need to show love to all people, regardless of their apparent state or condition.

There are many people walking around looking on the outside like everything is together and going well, while on the inside they are falling apart. We have to stop making people work so hard for love. That should not be the case. People should not have to be in complete despair before someone notices them. God's love does not work that way. Paul says in Romans 8, I am convinced that nothing shall separate us from the love of God. Regardless of the situation, regardless of whatever we may have done, God still loves us.

This man had been sitting in a season of waiting for thirty-eight years. It was a frustrating season; as when the angel comes and stirs the pool, he tries to make his way to the pool on his own and someone always manages to get the healing in front of him. He tries and tries to make it to his deliverance; but right when he is on the brink of his breakthrough the rug is slipped out from under him. For us it may be that we are starting to make progress on something, we begin to see our way out then something happens, and the struggle begins again.

The man answered Jesus' question by detailing all the reasons, excuses, and barriers he had to getting into the pool first. He was convinced his method of healing would be a pool of water, when the one who gives living water was standing right in front of him. But Jesus looked beyond this man's excuses and saw his need. Jesus did not leave this man where He found him. Jesus said to him "Rise, take up your bed and walk."

We do not have to stay in the state we are currently in. Through the power of Jesus Christ, we can rise. How long will you stay in the state you are in? What is holding you back? How many generations will be bound by the same habits and weaknesses? Jesus is asking today, "Do you want to be made well? In order to rise you must release whatever it is that's holding you back; give it to God. Confess those things with your mouth. Believe with your heart that Jesus is Lord and is able to elevate you. He will raise you out of your current state and will guide you forward to the path He has designed for you.

The Power to Heal in Many Ways

Foundational Scripture

Matthew 8: 1-13. When He had come
down from the mountain, great
multitudes followed Him. 2 And
behold, a leper came and worshiped
Him, saying, "Lord, if You are

willing, You can make me clean."
[3] Then Jesus put out His hand and
touched him, saying, "I am willing; be
cleansed." Immediately his
leprosy was cleansed. [4] And Jesus said
to him, "See that you tell no one; but
go your way, show yourself to the
priest, and offer the gift
that Moses commanded, as a
testimony to them." [5] Now when Jesus
had entered Capernaum, a centurion
came to Him, pleading with
Him, [6] saying, "Lord, my servant is
lying at home paralyzed, dreadfully
tormented." [7] And Jesus said to
him, "I will come and heal him."
[8] The centurion answered and said,
"Lord, I am not worthy that You
should come under my roof. But
only speak a word, and my servant
will be healed. [9] For I also am a man
under authority, having soldiers under
me. And I say to this one, 'Go,' and
he goes; and to another, 'Come,' and
he comes; and to my servant, 'Do
this,' and he does it." [10] When Jesus

heard it, He marveled, and said to those who followed, "Assuredly, I say to you, I have not found such great faith, not even in Israel! [11] And I say to you that many will come from east and west, and sit down with Abraham, Isaac, and Jacob in the kingdom of heaven. [12] But the sons of the kingdom will be cast out into outer darkness. There will be weeping and gnashing of teeth." [13] Then Jesus said to the centurion, "Go your way; and as you have believed, so let it be done for you." And his servant was healed that same hour.

The man with leprosy came to Jesus and said, "Lord if you are willing, you can make me clean." This man spoke of God's power and unfailing ability. There was no doubt, no question in the leper's spirit. He made a statement; he didn't ask a question. He knew that Jesus had the power and ability to make him clean. And Jesus healed him.

A centurion came to Jesus in Capernaum and asked that He heal his servant who was paralyzed and suffering. Jesus said He would go to the man's house and heal his servant. The centurion said he did not feel he was worthy for Jesus to come into his house. So, the centurion said to Jesus, "If you would just speak the word, I know my servant would be healed."

This is the faith we must have. The word of God has tremendous power. Through the death and resurrection of Jesus, and the gift of the Holy Spirit, we have the ability to access the power of God. There is healing power in the word of God.

The Bible says that life and death are in the power of the tongue. We may not be able to go into the schools everyday with our children. But by faith, if we speak the word and speak life, the word of God will travel into the school with our children and provide protection, favor and comfort for our children. We may not be able to go into the hospital room beyond visiting hours. But with faith in God's word, we can speak the word for healing to go forth. Jesus was touched by the faith of the centurion. Jesus said "Go! It will be done just as you believed it would." The centurion's servant was healed that same hour.

Jesus' words "It will be done just as you believed" are truly powerful. We must have a spirit of expectation. We must believe we have the victory. We must believe we are more than conquerors.

As we revisit Mark 4, wherein Jesus was in the boat with His disciples and a furious storm arose; The Bible says the storm came "without warning." So many times, it is the "un-forecasted" storms in our lives that causes the fear and doubt to come in, just as it did with the disciples. Jesus replied to their expression of fear by saying "You of little faith why are you so afraid." Jesus got up and calmed the storm. The men asked "What kind of man is this? Even the winds and waves obey him." That is my God!

God is able to change the course of the storm. As the winds start blowing, as lightening starts flashing, as thunder starts to roll, throw your hands up and say, "Father I stretch my hands to thee no other help I know." God can change the course, intensity, and nature of the storm. He is the God that even the winds and sea obey him. He is my God!

Protection from the Flames

Foundational Scripture
Daniel 3:15-30. Now if you are ready at the time, you hear the sound of the horn, flute, harp, lyre, and psaltery, in symphony with all kinds of music, and you fall down and worship the image

which I have made, good! But if you
do not worship, you shall be cast
immediately into the midst of a
burning fiery furnace. And who is the
god who will deliver you from my
hands?" 16 Shadrach, Meshach, and
Abed-Nego answered and said to the
king, "O Nebuchadnezzar, we have no
need to answer you in this matter. 17 If
that is the case, our God whom we
serve is able to deliver us from the
burning fiery furnace, and He will
deliver us from your hand, O
king. 18 But if not, let it be known to
you, O king, that we do not serve your
gods, nor will we worship the gold
image which you have set up." 19 Then
Nebuchadnezzar was full of fury, and
the expression on his face changed
toward Shadrach, Meshach, and Abed-
Nego. He spoke and commanded that
they heat the furnace seven times more
than it was usually heated. 20 And he
commanded certain mighty men of
valor who were in his army to bind
Shadrach, Meshach, and Abed-

Nego, and cast them into the burning
fiery furnace. [21] Then these men were
bound in their coats, their trousers,
their turbans, and their other garments,
and were cast into the midst of the
burning fiery furnace. [22] Therefore,
because the king's command was
urgent, and the furnace exceedingly
hot, the flame of the fire killed those
men who took up Shadrach, Meshach,
and Abed-Nego. [23] And these three
men, Shadrach, Meshach, and Abed-
Nego, fell down bound into the midst
of the burning fiery furnace. [24] Then
King Nebuchadnezzar was astonished;
and he rose in haste and spoke, saying
to his counselors, "Did we not cast
three men bound into the midst of the
fire?" They answered and said to the
king, "True, O king." [25] "Look!" he
answered, "I see four men
loose, walking in the midst of the fire;
and they are not hurt, and the form of
the fourth is like the Son of God."
[26] Then Nebuchadnezzar went near
the mouth of the burning fiery

furnace and spoke, saying, "Shadrach,
Meshach, and Abed-Nego, servants of
the Most High God, come out, and
come here." Then Shadrach, Meshach,
and Abed-Nego came from the midst
of the fire. 27 And the satraps,
administrators, governors, and the
king's counselors gathered together,
and they saw these men on whose
bodies the fire had no power; the hair
of their head was not singed nor were
their garments affected, and the smell
of fire was not on them.
28 Nebuchadnezzar spoke, saying,
"Blessed be the God of Shadrach,
Meshach, and Abed-Nego, who sent
His Angel and delivered His servants
who trusted in Him, and they have
frustrated the king's word, and yielded
their bodies, that they should not serve
nor worship any god except their own
God! 29 Therefore I make a decree that
any people, nation, or language which
speaks anything amiss against the God
of Shadrach, Meshach, and Abed-
Nego shall be cut in pieces, and their

houses shall be made an ash heap; because there is no other God who can deliver like this." [30] Then the king promoted Shadrach, Meshach, and Abed-Nego in the province of Babylon.

In these scriptures, we find a great demonstration of faith and protection. King Nebuchadnezzar had made a golden idol of himself. He set forth a law that mandated that at the time the music sounded everyone was to fall down and worship the golden image.

However, three young Hebrew boys, Shadrach, Meshach, and Abednego remembered the ten commandments, which are written in Exodus 20:3-17. The first commandment is, "You shall have no other gods before me. You shall not make for yourself a carved image. You shall not bow down to them or serve them." Therefore, this law that was established by King Nebuchadnezzar was clearly against the law of God.

Shadrach, Meshach, and Abednego had a choice to make: Do we serve God and suffer the wrath of man? Or do we serve man and suffer the wrath of God? They made the right decision. For once we choose to serve God, He will take care of the rest.

The wrath of man led them to the consequence of being thrown into the fiery furnace. Frustrated by their unshaken devotion to God, King Nebuchadnezzar order the furnace to be heated seven times the normal temperature. The flames were so hot that the men chosen to throw them into the furnace were killed. The three young Hebrew boys were bound and thrown in the furnace. But God acknowledged their faithfulness; and saw that they were being persecuted for righteousness' sake. He delivered them.

When the king looked in the furnace, he was shocked. In verse 25 he states, "Look, I see four men loose, walking in the midst of the fire; and they are not hurt, and the form of the fourth is like the Son of God." God allowed them to walk around in the midst of the fire and not be harmed.

When they came out of the fire they did not even smell like smoke. Not only did He empower them to do this; but He was there with them when they were in the middle of the flames. Those that looked in, saw that the men were not alone. They saw that although they had done everything they could to destroy the faithful followers of God, no weapon formed against them had prospered. God was powerful enough to protect Shadrach, Meshach, and Abednego from the flames that were hot enough to kill those who put them in the furnace.

We at times may find ourselves surrounded by the fires and trials of life. At times, these fiery trials may be due to unwise decisions or actions. But there are times where we can find ourselves in the middle of trials that have come for no other reason but to teach us something or to prepare us for a new phase in our calling. Regardless of the reason we may be in the middle of fiery trials, when we find ourselves there; we must remember we have access to an almighty and all-powerful God.

God is able to save us from the fires. But even if it is His will for us to endure the flames, He will not leave us nor forsake us. He will step into the fire with us to ensure we know, and others know, that He is our Savior, and He is our Protector. He is all-powerful. His power is not diminished due to temperature change. When things in your life heat up, He can shield you from it. He can enable you to not only withstand the heat, but you will come out not even smelling like smoke. You will not look like what you have been through. You will not talk like what you have been through. God uses His power to protect what he has created.

Protection from the Lions

Foundational Scripture

Daniel 6:1-28. It pleased Darius to set
over the kingdom one hundred and
twenty satraps, to be over the whole
kingdom; [2] and over these, three
governors, of whom Daniel was one,
that the satraps might give account to
them, so that the king would suffer no
loss. [3] Then this Daniel distinguished
himself above the governors and
satraps, because an excellent
spirit was in him; and the king gave
thought to setting him over the whole
realm. [4] So the governors and satraps
sought to find some charge against
Daniel concerning the kingdom; but
they could find no charge or fault,

because he was faithful; nor was there
any error or fault found in him. [5] Then
these men said, "We shall not find any
charge against this Daniel unless we
find it against him concerning the law
of his God." [6] So these governors and
satraps thronged before the king, and
said thus to him: "King Darius, live
forever! [7] All the governors of the
kingdom, the administrators and
satraps, the counselors and advisors,
have consulted together to establish a
royal statute and to make a firm decree,
that whoever petitions any god or man
for thirty days, except you, O king,
shall be cast into the den of
lions. [8] Now, O king, establish the
decree and sign the writing, so that it
cannot be changed, according to
the law of the Medes and Persians,
which does not alter." [9] Therefore
King Darius signed the written decree.
[10] Now when Daniel knew that the
writing was signed, he went home.
And in his upper room, with his
windows open toward Jerusalem, he

knelt down on his knees three times that day, and prayed and gave thanks before his God, as was his custom since early days. 11 Then these men assembled and found Daniel praying and making supplication before his God. 12 And they went before the king, and spoke concerning the king's decree: "Have you not signed a decree that every man who petitions any god or man within thirty days, except you, O king, shall be cast into the den of lions?" The king answered and said, "The thing is true, according to the law of the Medes and Persians, which does not alter." 13 So they answered and said before the king, "That Daniel, who is one of the captives from Judah, does not show due regard for you, O king, or for the decree that you have signed, but makes his petition three times a day." 14 And the king, when he heard these words, was greatly displeased with himself, and set his heart on Daniel to deliver him; and he labored till the going down of

the sun to deliver him. [15] Then these
men approached the king, and said to
the king, "Know, O king, that it is the
law of the Medes and Persians that no
decree or statute which the king
establishes may be changed." [16] So the
king gave the command, and they
brought Daniel and cast him into the
den of lions. But the king spoke,
saying to Daniel, "Your God, whom
you serve continually, He will deliver
you." [17] Then a stone was brought and
laid on the mouth of the den, and the
king sealed it with his own signet ring
and with the signets of his lords, that
the purpose concerning Daniel might
not be changed. [18] Now the king went
to his palace and spent the night
fasting; and no musicians were
brought before him. Also, his
sleep went from him. [19] Then the king
arose very early in the morning and
went in haste to the den of lions. [20] And
when he came to the den, he cried out
with a lamenting voice to Daniel. The
king spoke, saying to Daniel, "Daniel,

servant of the living God, has your God, whom you serve continually, been able to deliver you from the lions?" [21] Then Daniel said to the king, "O king, live forever! [22] My God sent His angel and shut the lions' mouths, so that they have not hurt me, because I was found innocent before Him; and also, O king, I have done no wrong before you." [23] Now the king was exceedingly glad for him and commanded that they should take Daniel up out of the den. So, Daniel was taken up out of the den, and no injury whatever was found on him, because he believed in his God. [24] And the king gave the command, and they brought those men who had accused Daniel, and they cast them into the den of lions—them, their children, and their wives; and the lions overpowered them, and broke all their bones in pieces before they ever came to the bottom of the den. [25] Then King Darius wrote: To all peoples, nations, and languages that

dwell in all the Earth: Peace be
multiplied to you. [26] I make a decree
that in every dominion of my
kingdom men must tremble and fear
before the God of Daniel. For He is the
living God, and steadfast forever; His
kingdom is the one which shall not
be destroyed, And His dominion shall
endure to the end. [27] He delivers and
rescues, And He works signs and
wonders in heaven and on Earth, who
has delivered Daniel from the power of
the lions. [28] So this Daniel prospered in
the reign of Darius and in the reign
of Cyrus the Persian.

The word of God says pray without ceasing. There was no law or king that could make Daniel turn from what God commands. Daniel stood firm on his faith. In Daniel 6, King Darius was manipulated by his administrators to issue a decree which stated that for thirty days anyone who prays to any god or any man other than King Darius would be thrown into the lion's den.

Once Daniel heard this, he didn't cry, he didn't fret, he wasn't worried or confused. Daniel knew exactly what he was going to do. Daniel went home into his upper room, opened his windows, knelt down on his knees and prayed. The prayers Daniel prayed were not prayers of woe and sorrow. Daniel prayed prayers of thanksgiving. In the midst of those plotting against him, Daniel gave thanks to God. Daniel knew that no weapon formed against him would prosper. So, while the weapons were being formed, he prayed. Once they launched the weapons, he prayed. At times we can get so caught up with what the enemy is doing, that we lose sight of what we ought to be doing, which is praising and thanking God.

Daniel chose, as did Shadrach, Meshach, and Abednego, to obey God. He was tossed into the lion's den. But God demonstrated his power of protection again. The next day the king rushed to the den to check to see what happened. He yelled into the den "Daniel, servant of the living God, has your God whom you serve continually been able to deliver you from the lions?"

Prior to Daniel being thrown into the den the king made a statement not a question. The night Daniel was thrown into the den, the king stated that the God who Daniel served continually will deliver him. However overnight, the king allowed the situation and circumstance in the natural change his statement to a question. What is your statement of faith? Prepare your statement of faith, your absolutes. The things you will walk in daily. Do not allow anything to change your statement of faith into a question.

After the King cried out to Daniel, Daniel responded and said, "My God sent His angel and shut the lions' mouths, so they have not hurt me." At times, you may find yourself surrounded by people who are seeking to devour you. They may be seeking to devour you with their words or their actions. God is able to protect you.

In verse 26, King Darius made a new decree. He stated, "I issue a decree that in every part of my kingdom; people must fear and reverence the God of Daniel. For He is the living God, and He endures forever; His kingdom will not be destroyed, His dominion will never end. He rescues and He saves; He performs signs and wonders in the heavens and on the Earth. He has rescued Daniel from the power of the lions." God's protection and deliverance of Daniel caused others to believe. God's power is unimaginable!

This is the reason that Daniel could not go thirty days without talking to and thanking God. God is too good. When I think of the goodness of Jesus and all that He's done for me my soul cries out Hallelujah! People can decree what they want, but I declare that my God is good, and He is worthy to be praised. I can't go thirty days or thirty minutes without saying "Thank You God!"

The Power to Guide

In Psalm 119:105, David says "Your word is a lamp to my feet and a light to my path." Without God's word we would remain lost in darkness. His word is a lamp to our feet, revealing to us the place in which we are currently standing. His word is also a light unto our path, showing us the path, we should take.

Parting of the Red Sea

Foundational Scripture

Exodus 14:5-21. Now it was told the king of Egypt that the people had fled, and the heart of Pharaoh and his servants was turned against the people;

and they said, "Why have we done this,
that we have let Israel go from serving
us?" [6] So he made ready his chariot
and took his people with him. [7] Also,
he took six hundred choice chariots,
and all the chariots of Egypt with
captains over every one of them. [8] And
the LORD hardened the heart of
Pharaoh king of Egypt, and he pursued
the children of Israel; and the children
of Israel went out with boldness. [9] So
the Egyptians pursued them, all the
horses and chariots of Pharaoh, his
horsemen and his army, and overtook
them camping by the sea beside Pi
Hahiroth, before Baal Zephon. [10] And
when Pharaoh drew near, the children
of Israel lifted their eyes, and behold,
the Egyptians marched after them. So,
they were very afraid, and the children
of Israel cried out to the LORD. [11] Then
they said to Moses, "Because there
were no graves in Egypt, have you
taken us away to die in the wilderness?
Why have you so dealt with us, to
bring us up out of Egypt? [12] Is this not

the word that we told you in Egypt,
saying, 'Let us alone that we may serve
the Egyptians'? For it would have
been better for us to serve the
Egyptians than that we should die in
the wilderness." [13] And Moses said to
the people, "Do not be afraid. Stand
still, and see the salvation of the LORD,
which He will accomplish for you
today. For the Egyptians whom you
see today, you shall see again no more
forever. [14] The LORD will fight for
you, and you shall hold your peace."
[15] And the LORD said to Moses, "Why
do you cry to Me? Tell the children of
Israel to go forward. [16] But lift up your
rod and stretch out your hand over the
sea and divide it. And the children of
Israel shall go on dry ground through
the midst of the sea. [17] And I indeed
will harden the hearts of the Egyptians,
and they shall follow them. So, I
will gain honor over Pharaoh and over
all his army, his chariots, and his
horsemen. [18] Then the Egyptians shall
know that I am the LORD, when I have

gained honor for Myself over Pharaoh, his chariots, and his horsemen." [19] And the Angel of God, who went before the camp of Israel, moved and went behind them; and the pillar of cloud went from before them and stood behind them. [20] So it came between the camp of the Egyptians and the camp of Israel. Thus, it was a cloud and darkness to the one, and it gave light by night to the other, so that the one did not come near the other all that night. [21] Then Moses stretched out his hand over the sea; and the LORD caused the sea to go back by a strong east wind all that night, and made the sea into dry land, and the waters were divided.

After being delivered from slavery, the Israelites found themselves facing yet another obstacle. Pharaoh and his army had followed them to the Red Sea. To a faithless person, it would seem that they were trapped. It seemed they would either drown in the sea or be killed by Pharaoh's army. However, God had not delivered them from slavery in Egypt just for them to perish in the sea. God provided a way of escape.

In verse 16, God gives Moses his instructions. God stated, "Lift up your rod, and stretch out your hand over the sea and divide it. And the children of Israel shall go on dry ground through the midst of the sea." Moses followed the instructions, and the power of God was again demonstrated. Verse 21 states, "Then Moses stretched out his hand over the sea; and God caused the sea to go back by a strong east wind all that night, and made the sea into dry land, and the waters were divided. So, the children of Israel went into the midst of the sea on the dry ground, and the waters were a wall to them on their right hand and on their left."

God then caused the waters to fall on the Egyptian army that were pursuing the Israelites and the Egyptian army drowned. God is powerful enough to provide a way of escape from all situations. He has the power to make a way out of no way.

Power to Make a Way

Foundational Scripture

Joshua 3:1-17. Then Joshua rose early
in the morning; and they set
out from Acacia Grove and came to
the Jordan, he and all the children of
Israel, and lodged there before they
crossed over. 2 So it was, after three
days, that the officers went through the
camp; 3 and they commanded the
people, saying, "When you see the ark
of the covenant of the LORD your
God, and the priests, the
Levites, bearing it, then you shall set
out from your place and go after
it. 4 Yet there shall be a space between
you and it, about two thousand cubits
by measure. Do not come near it, that
you may know the way by which you

must go, for you have not
passed this way before." [5] And Joshua
said to the people, "Sanctify
yourselves, for tomorrow
the LORD will do wonders among
you." [6] Then Joshua spoke to the
priests, saying, "Take up the ark of the
covenant and cross over before the
people." So, they took up the ark of the
covenant and went before the people.
[7] And the LORD said to Joshua, "This
day I will begin to exalt you in the sight
of all Israel, that they may know
that, as I was with Moses, so I will be
with you. [8] You shall command the
priests who bear the ark of the
covenant, saying, 'When you have
come to the edge of the water of the
Jordan, you shall stand in the Jordan.'
"[9] So Joshua said to the children of
Israel, "Come here, and hear the words
of the LORD your God." [10] And Joshua
said, "By this you shall know that the
living God is among you, and that He
will without fail drive out from before
you the Canaanites and the Hittites and

the Hivites and the Perizzites and the
Girgashites and the Amorites and the
Jebusites: 11 Behold, the ark of the
covenant of the Lord of all the Earth is
crossing over before you into the
Jordan. 12 Now therefore, take for
yourselves twelve men from the tribes
of Israel, one man from every
tribe. 13 And it shall come to pass, as
soon as the soles of the feet of the
priests who bear the ark of
the LORD, the Lord of all the Earth,
shall rest in the waters of the
Jordan, that the waters of the Jordan
shall be cut off, the waters that come
down from upstream, and they shall
stand as a heap." 14 So it was, when the
people set out from their camp to cross
over the Jordan, with the priests
bearing the ark of the covenant before
the people, 15 and as those who bore the
ark came to the Jordan, and the feet of
the priests who bore the ark dipped in
the edge of the water (for the Jordan
overflows all its banks during the
whole time of harvest), 16 that the

waters which came down from upstream stood still, and rose in a heap very far away at Adam, the city that is beside Zaretan. So, the waters that went down into the Sea of the Arabah, the Salt Sea, failed, and were cut off; and the people crossed over opposite Jericho.
[17] Then the priests who bore the ark of the covenant of the LORD stood firm on dry ground in the midst of the Jordan; and all Israel crossed over on dry ground, until all the people had crossed completely over the Jordan.

Another example of God making a way out of no way is found in Joshua chapter 3. In Joshua 3, the Israelites were at the Jordan river. They had to cross over the Jordan river to get to the land God had promised them. God told them to wait three days at the shore of the Jordan river. For three days, they watched the raging waters wondering how they were going to get across.

Sometimes to get to what God has for us, there may be seemingly insurmountable obstacles in the way. In those moments we may have to wait and be patient for the promise to come to fruition. We must evaluate what we do in the waiting period, when the waters are raging and the people around you may be worried, doubting, and complaining.

James tells us in James 1 to "count it all joy when you fall into various trials, knowing that the testing of your faith produces patience." We must have patience. But we need to have patience with faith so that we are not waiting in fear. We must have faith in God's word. In Matthew 17, Jesus tells us "If you have faith as small as a mustard seed, you can say to this mountain, 'Move from here to there,' and it will move. Nothing will be impossible for you." God once again made a way out of no way and enabled the Israelites to cross into what he had promised them.

The Power to Deliver

Foundational Scripture

Genesis 6:13-22. And God said to
Noah, "The end of all flesh has come
before Me, for the Earth is filled with
violence through them; and behold, I
will destroy them with the
Earth. [14] Make yourself an ark of
gopherwood; make rooms in the ark,
and cover it inside and outside with
pitch. [15] And this is how you shall
make it: The length of the ark shall
be three hundred cubits, its width fifty
cubits, and its height thirty
cubits. [16] You shall make a window for
the ark, and you shall finish it to a cubit
from above; and set the door of the ark
in its side. You shall make
it with lower, second, and
third decks. [17] And behold, I Myself
am bringing floodwaters on the Earth,

to destroy from under heaven all flesh
in which is the breath of life;
everything that is on the Earth
shall die. [18] But I will establish
My covenant with you; and you shall
go into the ark—you, your sons, your
wife, and your sons' wives with
you. [19] And of every living thing of all
flesh you shall bring two of
every sort into the ark, to
keep them alive with you; they shall be
male and female. [20] Of the birds after
their kind, of animals after their kind,
and of every creeping thing of the
Earth after its kind, two of
every kind will come to you to
keep them alive. [21] And you shall take
for yourself of all food that is eaten,
and you shall gather it to yourself; and
it shall be food for you and for them."
[22] Thus Noah did; according to all
that God commanded him, so he did.

In Genesis 6, God had decided to destroy the Earth by flood. He directed

Noah to build an ark that would save him and his family. God gave Noah very specific instructions on how to build the ark; and Noah obeyed God. At this point in time, it had never rained before. Noah was called to prepare for something new, something those around him could not imagine or understand. But in the midst of the doubters, in the midst of those that talked about him and mocked him, Noah had to focus on God's word and instruction. He had to be able to tune out the distraction, and press forward to do the work God called him to do. The rain was coming, and the ark needed to be built before the rain came.

Today God is calling us to build a spiritual structure that will be a shelter in the storms of life. It is a structure of salvation. God gave us the instructions through the word of God. We do not have to create our own instructions or come up with our own blueprint and list of necessary parts.

Proverbs 3 states "Trust in the Lord with all thine heart; and lean not unto thine own understanding. In all thy ways acknowledge Him, and He shall direct thy paths." We do not have to find a guide. God is our guide. God has the power to guide us to our deliverance and to living our lives fulfilling our purpose.

The Power to Resurrect

Foundational Scripture

John 11:38-44. Then Jesus, again groaning in Himself, came to the tomb. It was a cave, and a stone lay against
it. 39 Jesus said, "Take away the stone." Martha, the sister of him who was dead, said to Him, "Lord, by this time there is a stench, for he has
been dead four days." 40 Jesus said to her, "Did I not say to you that if you would believe you would see the glory
of God?" 41 Then they took away the stone from the place where the dead

man was lying. And Jesus lifted up His eyes and said, "Father, I thank You that You have heard Me. [42] And I know that You always hear Me, but because of the people who are standing by I said this, that they may believe that You sent Me." [43] Now when He had said these things, He cried with a loud voice, "Lazarus, come forth!" [44] And he who had died came out bound hand and foot with graveclothes, and his face was wrapped with a cloth. Jesus said to them, "Loose him, and let him go."

In John 11:38-44, God demonstrates his power over death. There was a man named Lazarus who was a friend of Jesus'; and Lazarus became sick. Lazarus' sisters, Mary and Martha went to Jesus to let Him know that Lazarus was sick. Jesus responded and said that the sickness will not end in death. But that it is for God's glory.

After hearing that Lazarus was sick,

Jesus stayed where He was for two more days. Then He headed back to Judea. Jesus said to the disciples "Our friend Lazarus has fallen asleep; but I am going there to wake him up." The disciples did not understand and said to Jesus, if he is just sleep, he will get better. Jesus clarified it for them by saying "Lazarus is dead, and for your sake I am glad I was not there, so that you may believe."

They traveled to where Lazarus was buried. Once they arrived, they found that Lazarus had been buried for four days already. When Martha heard that Jesus was close, she went to meet him and said to Jesus "if you had been here, my brother would not have died." Jesus said to her "Your brother will rise again." Jesus goes on to say, "I am the resurrection and the life."

When Jesus gets to the tomb, Jesus instructs them to roll the stone away from Lazarus' tomb. Martha begins to complain and tell Jesus that Lazarus has been dead for four days, and that his body would smell. In verse 40, Jesus responds to her by saying, "Did I not say to you that if you would believe you would see the glory of God?" And in verse 43, he commands Lazarus to come forth, and Lazarus did. Jesus raised Lazarus from the dead. God received the glory from this miracle. God's power to resurrect was shown.

The Crucifixion and Resurrection

Foundational Scripture

Matthew 27:11-66. Now Jesus stood
before the governor. And the
governor asked Him, saying, "Are
You the King of the Jews?" Jesus said
to him, "It is as you say." 12 And while
He was being accused by the chief
priests and elders, He answered
nothing. 13 Then Pilate said to
Him, "Do You not hear how many
things they testify against

You?" [14] But He answered him not
one word, so that the governor
marveled greatly. Taking the Place of
Barabbas [15] Now at the feast the
governor was accustomed to releasing
to the multitude one prisoner whom
they wished. [16] And at that time they
had a notorious prisoner called
Barabbas. [17] Therefore, when they had
gathered together, Pilate said to them,
"Whom do you want me to release to
you? Barabbas, or Jesus who is called
Christ?" [18] For he knew that they had
handed Him over because of envy.
[19] While he was sitting on the
judgment seat, his wife sent to him,
saying, "Have nothing to do with that
just Man, for I have suffered many
things today in a dream because of
Him." [20] But the chief priests and
elders persuaded the multitudes that
they should ask for Barabbas and
destroy Jesus. [21] The governor
answered and said to them, "Which of
the two do you want me to release to
you?" They said, "Barabbas!" [22] Pilate

said to them, "What then shall I do
with Jesus who is called Christ?"
They all said to him, "Let Him be
crucified!" 23 Then the governor
said, "Why, what evil has He done?"
But they cried out all the more,
saying, "Let Him be crucified!"
24 When Pilate saw that he could not
prevail at all, but rather that a tumult
was rising, he took water and
washed his hands before the
multitude, saying, "I am innocent of
the blood of this just Person. You
see to it." 25 And all the people
answered and said, "His blood be on
us and on our children." 26 Then he
released Barabbas to them; and
when he had scourged Jesus, he
delivered Him to be crucified.

The Soldiers Mock Jesus

27 Then the soldiers of the governor
took Jesus into the Praetorium and
gathered the whole garrison around
Him. 28 And they stripped Him
and put a scarlet robe on

Him. 29 When they had twisted a
crown of thorns, they put it on His
head, and a reed in His right hand.
And they bowed the knee before Him
and mocked Him, saying, "Hail, King
of the Jews!" 30 Then they spat on
Him, and took the reed and struck
Him on the head. 31 And when they
had mocked Him, they took the robe
off Him, put His own clothes on
Him, and led Him away to be
crucified.

The King on a Cross

32 Now as they came out, they found a
man of Cyrene, Simon by name. Him
they compelled to bear His
cross. 33 And when they had come to a
place called Golgotha, that is to say,
Place of a Skull, 34 they gave
Him sour wine mingled with gall to
drink. But when He had tasted it, He
would not drink. 35 Then they
crucified Him, and divided His
garments, casting lots, that it might be
fulfilled which was spoken by the

prophet: "They divided My garments
among them, And for My clothing
they cast lots."36 Sitting down, they
kept watch over Him there. 37 And
they put up over His head the
accusation written against Him:

THIS IS JESUS THE KING OF THE
JEWS.

38 Then two robbers were crucified
with Him, one on the right and
another on the left. 39 And those who
passed by blasphemed Him, wagging
their heads 40 and saying, "You who
destroy the temple and build it in
three days, save Yourself! If You are
the Son of God, come down from the
cross." 41 Likewise the chief priests
also, mocking with the scribes and
elders, said, 42 "He saved others;
Himself He cannot save. If He is the
King of Israel, let Him now come
down from the cross, and we will
believe Him. 43 He trusted in God; let
Him deliver Him now if He will have
Him; for He said, 'I am the Son of

God.'" [44] Even the robbers who were
crucified with Him reviled Him with
the same thing.

Jesus Dies on the Cross

[45] Now from the sixth hour until the
ninth hour there was darkness over all
the land. [46] And about the ninth
hour Jesus cried out with a loud voice,
saying, "Eli, Eli, lama sabachthani?"
that is, "My God, My God, why have
You forsaken Me?" [47] Some of those
who stood there, when they
heard that, said, "This Man is calling
for Elijah!" [48] Immediately one of
them ran and took a
sponge, filled it with sour wine and
put it on a reed, and offered it to Him
to drink. [49] The rest said, "Let Him
alone; let us see if Elijah will come to
save Him." [50] And Jesus cried out
again with a loud voice and yielded
up His spirit. [51] Then, behold, the veil
of the temple was torn in two from
top to bottom; and the Earth quaked,
and the rocks were split, [52] and the

graves were opened; and many bodies
of the saints who had fallen asleep
were raised; 53 and coming out of the
graves after His resurrection, they
went into the holy city and appeared
to many. 54 So when the centurion and
those with him, who were guarding
Jesus, saw the earthquake and the
things that had happened, they feared
greatly, saying, "Truly this was the
Son of God!" 55 And many
women who followed Jesus from
Galilee, ministering to Him, were
there looking on from afar, 56 among
whom were Mary Magdalene, Mary
the mother of James and Joses, and
the mother of Zebedee's sons. Jesus
Buried in Joseph's Tomb
57 Now when evening had come, there
came a rich man from Arimathea,
named Joseph, who himself had also
become a disciple of Jesus. 58 This
man went to Pilate and asked for the
body of Jesus. Then Pilate
commanded the body to be given to
him. 59 When Joseph had taken the

body, he wrapped it in a clean linen
cloth, [60] and laid it in his new tomb
which he had hewn out of the rock;
and he rolled a large stone against the
door of the tomb and departed. [61] And
Mary Magdalene was there, and the
other Mary, sitting opposite the tomb.

Pilate Sets a Guard

[62] On the next day, which followed the
Day of Preparation, the chief priests
and Pharisees gathered together to
Pilate, [63] saying, "Sir, we remember,
while He was still alive, how that
deceiver said, 'After three days I will
rise.' [64] Therefore command that the
tomb be made secure until the third
day, lest His disciples come by night
and steal Him away, and say to the
people, 'He has risen from the dead.'
So, the last deception will be worse
than the first." [65] Pilate said to them,
"You have a guard; go your way,
make it as secure as you know
how." [66] So they went and made the

tomb secure, sealing the stone and setting the guard.

Jesus was shifting the corrupt religious and organizational structures, methods, and practices that were existing at that time. There was a plot launched against Jesus to try to condemn him. One of Jesus' disciples took part in this plot and betrayed Jesus to turn him over to the authorities. In Matthew 27, Jesus was brought before Pilate to answer the charges, Jesus did not say a word to Pilate, the chief priests or the elders.

When people accuse us and speak evil things against us, we should not be overcome with a need to convince others. Let our walk and our work speak for us. Let Jesus take care of the rest.

Pilate brought Jesus and Barabbas, a notorious criminal and murderer, before the crowd and asked which prisoner they would want released. Putting common sense aside and being clouded by evil, the crowd chose Barabbas to be released. The crowd asked for Jesus to be crucified. Pilate then washed his hands of it and told the crowd, "I am innocent of this man's blood. It is your responsibility."

The people answered, "Let his blood be on us and on our children." Unbeknownst to them, they were actually fulfilling prophesy in this wrong and despicable act, so that which they stated can come to fruition. This action had to take place so that Jesus' blood could cover them and their children. It is through His sacrifice and humility that His blood has the power to cover us today.

They then led Jesus to the Praetorium, the governor's official residence in Jerusalem and surrounded Him. They then proceeded to torture Him. They beat Him, spit on Him, made Him a crown out of thorns and pressed it into His skull, as they continued to beat Him with a staff. They led Him to Golgotha where He would be crucified.

As horrific as the torture of Jesus Christ was, every sin we commit is represented by this torture. Every lie is another crack of the whip. Every immoral act is another hateful remark. Many people mocked Him as He hung on the cross. They were saying "come down and save yourself." But instead, He made the choice to stay there, endure the mocking, endure the pain, and save all of us.

Once Jesus died, the veil (curtain) in the temple tore into two pieces. There was an earthquake; and tombs broke open. The centurion and those guarding Jesus saw everything that had happened, and they said, "truly this was the Son of God." Even after all the miracles that Jesus performed, it took all of this for them to recognize who He was.

To ensure that the disciples did not steal the body of Jesus and falsely claim that He rose from the dead, they put a seal on the stone covering the entrance to the tomb. They also posted a guard at the tomb. Despite all their efforts, they could not stop the will of God. They could try to bury Him, seal it, and guard it, but they could not stop it! Jesus was raised from the dead! He is alive! He is alive Hallelujah!

He is Risen

Foundational Scripture
Acts 2:22-25. "Men of Israel, hear these words: Jesus of Nazareth, a Man attested by God to you by miracles, wonders, and signs which God did through Him in your midst, as you yourselves also know [23] Him, being delivered by the determined purpose

and foreknowledge of God, you have
taken by lawless hands, have
crucified, and put to death; 24 whom
God raised up, having loosed
the pains of death, because it was not
possible that He should be held by
it. 25 For David says concerning Him:
'I foresaw the LORD always before
my face, For He is at my right hand,
that I may not be shaken.

In Acts 2:22-25 Peter speaks about Jesus and states, "Jesus of Nazareth was a man accredited by God to you by miracles, wonders and signs, which God did among you through Him, as you yourselves know. This man was handed over to you by God's set purpose and foreknowledge; and you, with the help of wicked men, put Him to death by nailing Him to the cross. But God raised Him from the dead, freeing Him from the agony of death, because it was impossible for death to keep its hold on Him." When Jesus was on the Earth, he endured all the negativity this world has to offer. He experienced loss, rejection, betrayal, pain, and anguish. He was beaten, tortured, crucified, and buried. But HE ROSE! He rose from the dead. The fact that He rose is amazing. The fact that He rose is awesome. The fact that He rose is miraculous. But what is most incredible is what happened when He rose. When He rose, He rose with all power in His hands. God has truly demonstrated his power over death.

There is a song that speaks about Jesus' resurrection from Jesus' point of view. The song lyrics state "Go ahead mock my name. My love for you is still the same. God ahead and bury me. But very soon I will be free. Cause I'll rise again. No power on Earth can keep me down. Yes, I'll rise again. Death can't keep me in the ground." No matter how far you may feel buried by your situation or buried by others' limitations they may put on you.

Please understand that the blood of Jesus reaches far and wide. Stir up the resurrection power of Jesus that is within you. That power will allow us to stand and say, "Go ahead and mock my name, talk about me, try to put limitations on me. Go ahead and form your weapons. But I will rise. Through Christ my Savior, I will rise. No power on this Earth can keep me down, because I have the spirit of the resurrected savior within me. I will rise."

God is all-powerful. There is nothing too hard for Him. If we simply believe in God and give Him control, He will demonstrate His power in our lives.

Since God is able to allow Shadrach, Meshach, and Abednego to walk in the midst of flames and not be harmed, is there any doubt that he can sustain us through the fires and trials of life? Since God is capable of shutting the mouths of lions so that no harm would befall Daniel, why would we doubt that he could shut the mouths of co-workers, classmates, or doubters who may speak evil against us? If God is able to speak to the wind and the waves and produce peace, is there any doubt that he is capable of calming the storms in our lives? If God parted the Red Sea so that the Israelites could escape the Egyptian army, is there any doubt that he could provide a way of escape from our problems and situations? Since God is able to multiply two fish and five loaves of bread and feed over 5,000 people, order the ravens to deliver food to Elijah, provide an unlimited supply of flour and oil to the obedient widow; how can we doubt that he is capable of providing financial stability, food, clothing, and shelter for our families? Since God has demonstrated his power over death, why do we doubt his healing power and the power to resurrect our dreams and goals? We must learn to trust God, for it is through faith that his power is demonstrated.

Activating the Power of God

Life is full of battles. We, in Christ, know that the war is already won. Through Christ, we have the victory. But along the way to victory there are battles, storms, and trials. In John 16:33, Jesus tells us "In this life you will have tribulations but be of good cheer I have overcome the world." We are not left to fight battles alone. We have access to the power of the Almighty God. There are three things we can use to activate the power of God – the Word of God, Faith, and Prayer.

Paul tells us in Ephesians 6 that the sword of the spirit is the word of God. The Bible provides the strategies we need to defeat the enemy's attempts to steal, kill, and destroy. We must meditate on His word day and night, so that we can fully understand the strategies we need.

The power of prayer lies within the power of the one we are praying to. We have to spend time with God to know His identity. In the word of God, He tells us that He is alpha and omega. He tells us that He is the way the truth and the life. He tells us that He is the God that heals us.

When we read and study the accounts and experiences in His word, we will see that: David tells us that He is a shepherd (Psalms 23). Noah tells us that He is a savior (Genesis 6-8). Moses tells us that He is a deliverer (Exodus 3-14); and Daniel tells us that He is a protector (Daniel 3; Daniel 6). The woman with the issue of blood tells us that he is a healer (Mark 5).
But as I go beyond simply reading the Bible, to meditating on the Bible and its application in my life; I will tell

you that He is whatever you need him to be. He is a way maker. He is a burden bearer. He is a provider. As the songwriter said, "Jesus, Jesus, Jesus He is the Answer."

Once we study His word and meditate on how He has shown up in our lives, we will know who he is. We must then build and use our faith in Him. The faith you have in Him is strengthened by your exposure to Him and His track record. It is strengthened by the prayers He has answered. It's strengthened by the miracles He has performed. When you reflect on His goodness, you will find that you can trust Him. You will find that He is faithful. Through our experiences and spending time with God, we will learn that if God says it's going to rain, you better get out and begin building an ark, because the rain is coming! You can count on Him!

Prayer does not work without faith. We saw this in one of the situations we reviewed in the previous section about the power to heal. This situation was where centurion that came to Jesus and asked God to heal His servant. The centurion's response to Jesus' agreement to come to His house was, "I am not worthy for you to come to my home, but if you would just speak the word, I know he will be healed". The centurion had faith and came to Jesus when his servant was too sick and too weak to go to Jesus for himself. Jesus healed his servant. We can also access the power of God through standing in the gap for others.

There are times we can face things in life that can hit us so hard and can take so much out of us that it can sometimes become hard to pray. There are times where we have prayed for things so long without seeing things turnaround; that our faith starts to waver. In those moments, it is so important to have those around us who can clock in and pray with faith for us. That is the power of prayer when it is activated by faith.

In James 3, it says "Is any one of you in trouble? He should pray. Is anyone happy? Let him sing songs of praise. Is anyone of you sick? He should call the elders of the church to pray over him and anoint him. And the prayer offered in faith will make the sick person well; the Lord will raise him up."

God is all-knowing. He already knows our condition and what we need. So, when I am praying to God, I do not pray to God to inform Him of my situation, as if He does not know what I am facing. But when I pray, I am expressing my dependence on Him and my faith in Him. I am not praying to let God know I have a problem, I am praying and saying Father God I know that you are aware of this battle I am facing. But I need you to know that I am coming to you saying "Lord I surrender ALL to you. I am fully dependent on you to help me to face these battles. I cannot do this on my own."

We cannot fight these battles of life by ourselves. But with the weapon of prayer, powered by faith and the sword of the spirit, which is the word of God, we can live victoriously.

There's a hymn of the church that I think about when I think about prayer. The song says: "I must tell Jesus all of my trials; I cannot bear these burdens alone." But then a turnaround happens, and the song goes on to say that "In my distress He kindly will help me. He ever loves and cares for His own." Once we have a little talk with Jesus, a turnaround can take place. A break-through can happen.

Prayer, with faith and the word of God, enables us to access the power of God to allow us to fulfill God's will for our lives.

Nutrient 3- Promise

The Intention of This Nutrient:

In Psalms 23, David said, "The Lord is my shepherd I shall not want." God is our shepherd, and He provides all we need. There are many promises that He gives us. But if we are unaware of the promises or of what our part in the promise is than we can live life reaching for things we already have access to.

Many organizations offer benefits and incentives to their employees. Some organizations offer to pay for educational pursuits or offer discounts on various products and services. If employees are unaware of these offers, they may spend time searching or go to great extremes to try to gain these benefits that the organization has made available to them. God has promised us a number of blessings and provisions in His word. Yet we often spend a lot of time, energy, and resources trying to gain peace, mercy, and other things we need that God has already promised to give us. We must hold up our end of the covenant and He is faithful to keep His promises.

The promise nutrient is intended to provide the victorious posture of knowing that we have access to blessing and favor through our covenant relationship with God through Christ. God does not lie. His promises are firm. If we do our part, He is faithful to His word.

In Isaiah 55:11 God says, "So shall My word be that goes forth from My mouth; It shall not return to Me void, but it shall accomplish what I please, and it shall prosper in the thing for which I sent it." Every promise that God makes, every word that He speaks, He has and will fulfill. We must be willing to meet the requirements to earn the benefits of the promise.

So often, we want to experience the joy of the resurrection without enduring the suffering of the cross. But we must keep in mind, as Dr. Martin Luther King Jr. stated, "Good Friday comes before Easter. Before the crown we wear, there is a cross we must bear," God never asks "too much." The costs never outweigh the benefits. Jesus paid the ultimate price. Therefore, if we want the promises of God, we must meet the requirements He clearly states in his word.

Prosperity and Protection

Foundational Scripture
Malachi 3:10-12. Bring all the tithes into the storehouse, that there may be food in My house, and try Me now in this," Says the Lord of hosts, "If I will

not open for you the windows of heaven and pour out for you such blessing that there will not be room enough to receive it. [11] "And I will rebuke the devourer for your sakes, so that he will not destroy the fruit of your ground, nor shall the vine fail to bear fruit for you in the field," Says the Lord of hosts; [12] "And all nations will call you blessed, for you will be a delightful land," says the Lord of hosts.

Verse 10 states, "Bring all the tithes into the storehouse, that there may be food in My house, and try Me now in this, "says the Lord of hosts, "If I will not open for you the windows of heaven and pour out for you such blessing that there will not be room enough to receive it." This is a promise. In these verses God says try it, prove me. The only thing He requires to receive the promises of prosperity and protection is that we pay our tithes.

Our tithes are a mere 10% of what God has graciously blessed us with. This is not just financial, we are to give our first fruits, our best in our time, energy, and resources to God. It is God's anyway! The Bible says, "The Earth is the Lord's and the fullness thereof."

If we do our part, God says that He will open up the windows of heaven. He will not only show us our riches in heaven, but He will show us that which He has purposed for us to have here on Earth. Verses 11 and 12 state, "And I will rebuke the devourer for your sakes, so that he will not destroy the fruit of your ground, nor shall the vine fail to bear fruit for you in the field," Says the Lord of hosts; and all nations will call you blessed, for you will be a delightful land," says the Lord of hosts." God offers this protection of prosperity for tithers.

In Genesis 25:30-33 Jacob cons Esau

out of his birthright. In Genesis 27:18-30, Jacob cons Isaac into giving him his blessing. But, in Genesis 28:11-22 Jacob has a dream. He awakes from his dream a redeemed man. In Genesis 28:22 Jacob states, "And this stone which I have set as a pillar shall be God's house, and of all that You give me I will surely give a tenth to You."

From this point on, Jacob was a tither. He was now entitled to the promises of Malachi 3:10-12. God then sent Jacob to get the blessings that God had purposed for him. He traveled to the house of Laban. He married Laban's daughter and worked for Laban. In Genesis 30:29-43, Jacob and Laban work out his payment for all the work he is doing. It was agreed that Jacob would receive the spotted and speckled sheep (which is normally an extremely small portion). But God protects the prosperity of the tither.

God shows Jacob how to obtain his

prosperity and Jacob obeyed. God told Jacob to wave a speckled branch over the sheep at their drinking place. And in Genesis 30:39 it states, "So the flocks conceived before the rods, and the flocks brought forth streaked, speckled, and spotted." Therefore, Jacob's flocks became numerous; and he became a wealthy man. If we are obedient and pay our tithes and offerings, He will not only grant us prosperity; but He will protect our prosperity.

The Promise of Protection

Foundational Scripture

Exodus 12:12-13. 'For I will pass through the land of Egypt on that night and will strike all the firstborn in the land of Egypt, both man and beast; and against all the gods of Egypt I will execute judgment: I am the Lord. [13] Now the blood shall be a sign for you on the houses where you are. And when I see the blood, I will pass over you; and the plague shall not be on you to destroy you when I strike the land of Egypt.

The Israelites were enslaved in Egypt. They had cried out to God, and He heard their cry. Deliverance was on the way. God sent Moses to lead His people out of Egypt into freedom. But it was a process. God had sent a series of plagues in Egypt to demonstrate to Pharaoh that God was all powerful and was sovereign. There were many plagues that Egypt experienced. There was a plague where water was turned to blood, a plague of frogs, insects, sickness - boils, a hails storm, and darkness. But the last plague was to be the deadliest of them all. The first born in every household in Egypt would be killed, as death swept through the land.

However, God prepared a way of salvation for the Israelites. The blood of a lamb would save them. They were to spread the blood of the lamb over the top and sides of the door of their homes. The Israelites were to stay inside their homes as death passed over the land. In Exodus 12, God instructed Moses to tell the people that "the blood of the lamb will be a sign for you on the houses where you are, and when I see the blood, this plague will pass over you when I strike Egypt." When God saw the blood over the houses of the Israelites, He spared them.

The world today is very corrupt. There is little reverence or obedience to God. As such, there are also plagues which exists today (drought, drugs, disease, poverty, etc.). God's promise still holds true. Therefore, it is vital that we keep our families under the blood of Jesus. For, there is protection under the blood. There is healing under the blood. There is salvation under the blood. There is grace and mercy under the blood.

There is deliverance under the blood. We must pray with and for our families. We must read the word of God together. We must do all we can to develop our families' relationships with God.

The Promise of Life

Foundational Scripture

Ephesians 6:1-3. Children, obey your parents in the Lord, for this is
right. 2 "Honor your father and mother," which is the first
commandment with promise: 3 "that it may be well with you, and you may live long on the Earth."

The Bible states that children need to obey their parents in the Lord, for this is right. This is the first commandment with promise. The promise is "that it may be well with you, and you may live long on the Earth." If we are unable to obey our parents who are here in the flesh with us on Earth, how can we obey God who we cannot see? In Deuteronomy 28:1-13 the blessings of obedience are detailed. Deuteronomy 28:15-68 details the curse of disobedience. Truly, obedience is better than sacrifice.

God promises long life to those who honor and obey their parents in the Lord. God is to be the head of the household. Therefore, if the word of our parents flows from God through our parents, how dare we question, talk back, disobey, or disrespect the vessels God has chosen to use. He often speaks through our parents to give us the words we need to hear. It is very important that we keep our relationship with God right, for then we will be in agreement when God speaks through our parents.

When we stray from the path of righteousness the Godly words of our parents may seem unfair, not understanding, and unjust. But the devil is a liar. The devil would have children believe that because their parents tell them no, that their parents are not "in the Lord." Satan will try to make it seem as though our parents are unjust and therefore not worthy of being used by God to speak wisdom to us. But once again, the devil is a liar. If we ever have doubt or questions regarding what our parents instruct us to do, we should obey God. We should always obey God.

God knew us before we were born. Jeremiah 1:4-5 states, "Before I formed you in the womb, I knew you; Before you were born, I sanctified you; I ordained you a prophet to the nations." He knew who we were, and he chose our parents. He matched us to the parents that we needed for us to fulfill our purpose. God holds our parents accountable for the way in which they raise their children. But it is not for us to judge or determine that our parents are not doing as God commands. Our parents may not be perfect, but every experience we have is for a purpose. We are consistently being prepared and molded for our calling.

We are responsible for our lives and our souls. We are responsible for the choices that we make. We must study the word of God to be able to discern what is “in the Lord” and what is not. Our ultimate guide is God and His word. The Bible says to, "obey your parents in the Lord, for this is right. "Honor your father and mother," which is the first commandment with promise: "that it may be well with you, and you may live long on the Earth." Now we must make the choice whether to obey God or follow our own foolish thinking. We have already seen how God rewards obedience. This is not a hard choice to make. Children, obey and honor your parents!

The Beatitudes

Foundational Scripture
Matthew 5:3-12. "Blessed are the
poor in spirit, for theirs is the
kingdom of heaven.[4] Blessed are those
who mourn, for they shall be
comforted. [5] Blessed are the meek,
for they shall inherit the Earth.
[6] Blessed are those who hunger and
thirst for righteousness, for they shall
be filled. [7] Blessed are the merciful,
for they shall obtain mercy.
[8] Blessed are the pure in heart,
for they shall see God.
[9] Blessed are the peacemakers, for
they shall be called sons of God.
[10] Blessed are those who are
persecuted for righteousness' sake, for
theirs is the kingdom of heaven.
[11] Blessed are you when they revile
and persecute you and say all kinds
of evil against you falsely for My
sake. [12] Rejoice and be exceedingly
glad, for great is your reward in

heaven, for so they persecuted the prophets who were before you.

Jesus had gone throughout Galilee preaching, teaching, and healing all kinds of illness and disease. Word of this spread quickly and crowds of people began following Him. In Matthew 5, when Jesus saw the crowd gather, he took the opportunity to preach and teach them.

He starts the message by revealing to the people how to be blessed. Being blessed goes far beyond being happy. It goes beyond the absence of current hardship. To be blessed is to have access to extensive favor, power, and spiritual joy. Being blessed is about the access that you have. This access is not granted due to your circumstance or your stature in life. It is granted by grace. For by grace are we saved; and through salvation we have access to the power of the almighty god.

The beginning of this sermon that Jesus preaches is commonly referred to as "The Beatitudes". Through this passage, Jesus provides clear instructions on the way in which we can be blessed. He also reveals the journey to be blessed. The beatitudes consist of a journey of eight steps. Let's begin this journey.

Matthew 5:3 states "Blessed are the poor in spirit for theirs is the kingdom of heaven." On the path to being blessed, the first step is to recognize that you need God. The opposite of being poor in spirit is being or thinking that you are self-sufficient and can get through this life on your own. Being poor in spirit means that you recognize that on your own, there is a lack, and a need. As we reviewed in the Power to Heal section, in Mark 5 there was a woman that had a bleeding issue for twelve years. She had been under doctor's care for years. She had spent a lot of money and was not getting any better. In fact, she was getting worse. When she heard that Jesus was coming through, she recognized that she had a need. She recognized that she was lacking something. She was not whole; so, she made her way to Jesus. Though the path was crowded with people, though she knew it wouldn't be a nice face to face lunch meeting to discuss her issue; driven by the criticality of her need, she pushed through the crowd to touch the hem of Jesus' garment. She was then healed.

Oftentimes we spend so much time, money, and energy trying to solve things on our own. This world teaches that you should be self-sufficient. To acknowledge a need and lack is seen as weakness in our current culture. But Jesus said blessed are the poor in spirit. Blessed are those that recognize they need Him. Blessed are they that are willing to press their way through the crowd of distractions and ill advice to reach Jesus. Blessed are they who press through those saying, "You don't need anybody else. You got this." Blessed are those that know they need to be on their knees saying it's me O Lord. I am standing in the need of prayer. I am lacking right now. For years I have been dealing with this issue. For years I have not had joy. For years I have felt all alone. I am in need. I can't do it on my own. If I can just touch you, Jesus. If I can just touch a piece of your garment.

When the needs get to be serious enough, you have no problem falling to your knees. When you get to a point that you cannot fake or hide it anymore. In 2 Corinthians 12, God is speaking to Paul and said, "My grace is sufficient for you; for my power is made perfect in weakness." Paul then says, "This is why for Christ's sake I delight in weaknesses, insults, in hardships, in persecution, in difficulties, for when I am weak, I am strong." Blessed are the poor in spirit for theirs is the kingdom of heaven.

Matthew 5:4 states "Blessed are those that mourn, for they will be comforted." Once we recognize our sin, there is a realization that we have wronged God which brings about a sadness or mourning. But that is just the first half of this verse. We must realize and feel sorrowful for our sins. But we should not get stuck in that sorrow and guilt. Jesus says, "Blessed are they that mourn for they shall be comforted."

In Luke 15 is the story of the prodigal son. There was a man with two sons. His youngest son came to him one day and asked for his inheritance. The father gave it to him, and the young son went to a distant country and spent all of his inheritance. He was partying and living wild. There is a cost to that lifestyle, and the cost is more than just money.

The young son soon found his inheritance was gone. His friends were gone. His joy was gone. His security was gone. His peace was gone. He was poor in spirit. At the point that he ran out of money, a famine hit the land. This young son was now in need. This was not a state that he was used to being in. He went and got a job where his first task was to feed and care for some pigs. One day as he was feeding the pigs, his need and hunger was so great that it brought him to his knees. His hunger overcame him to the point that he began to look at the slop the pigs were eating, and he began to want it.

He came to his senses. He realized that he had wronged his father and it hurt him. He recognized how far he had fallen. He felt unworthy to even be considered a son. He was truly sorrowful and in mourning. He decided to go back to his father and offer to work for him as a servant.

In this state of mourning over his wrongdoing, he returned home. But when his father saw him far off, he was filled with compassion. He got his best robe, ring, and sandals to adorn him and had a feast for him. Though the son was saddened and mourning because of his wrongdoing, in the end he was comforted. Blessed are they that mourn for they shall be comforted.

The Bible says all have sinned and fallen short of the glory of God. All have sinned. But not everyone is sorry for their sin. There are some that are living a life of sin, not thinking or aware of the sacrifice that was made for their salvation. There are those who are living in sin without considering the choice God made to send His only son to endure the required torture, pain, and death to pay for our sins. Some people are able to live in sin and not think about the physical and emotional abuse Jesus had to undergo. Some people do not consider the death He had to experience –a crown of thorns pressed into His head, a spear thrust into His side, bones broken, being nailed to the cross all for our sin.

But for those who recognize our wrongdoing and acknowledge the sacrifice Jesus made, there is a comfort. Weeping may endure for a night, but joy comes in the morning. Jesus rose from the dead with ALL power in His hands. In John 14, Jesus said I will not leave you comfortless. He said I will pray to the father, and he shall give you a comforter that will abide with you forever. Blessed are they that mourn for they shall be comforted.

Matthew 5:5 states "Blessed are the meek for they will inherit the Earth."

We must recognize God's sovereignty. This world professes that you must demonstrate your power, particularly your power over others. But Jesus says blessed are the meek. Being meek does not mean that you do not have power. Being meek means you have power or strength under perfect control.

Numbers 12:3 states "Now the man Moses was very meek above all the men, which were upon the face of the Earth. But Moses was a great leader. He had to face Pharoah to have the Israelites released from slavery. Moses recognized God's sovereignty. He listened and obeyed God. He submitted to God's will.

Once we recognize our lack and that we cannot save ourselves, we acknowledge our sins and repent of them; we must then become meek, by submitting to God's will. When we are in God's will, He fights our battles for us.

In Numbers 12, Miriam and Aaron, Moses' siblings, were talking about Moses. They did not like his wife and did not like the spotlight he was given. God then called all three of them, Moses, Aaron, and Miriam, out of the tent of meeting. God then came down in a pillar of cloud and asked Aaron and Miriam to step forward. He then asserted that He called Moses and appeared to Moses, face to face. He told them they should be afraid to speak against Moses. God then left, and when He did Miriam immediately became leprous. They then pleaded for Moses' forgiveness.

If you do what God ask you to do and submit to His will, God will take care of the rest. Jesus teaches us in Matthew 6 to "Seek ye first the kingdom of God and his righteousness, and all these things will be added unto you." Blessed are the meek for they will inherit the Earth.

Verse 6 says "Blessed are those who hunger and thirst after righteousness, for they shall be filled." Hunger and thirst are not a one-time need. It is an ongoing daily need in order to survive.

As we review the events captured in Daniel 6 again, King Darius' officials became jealous as Daniel was given the authority to run the kingdom. So, they came up with a plan. They got King Darius to create a law that would not allow anyone to pray to or worship any god or man except for King Darius. If they do, they will be thrown into the den of lions. But Daniel had an unquenchable hunger and thirst for God's righteousness. So, he continued to pray to God. Once the other officials discovered Daniel still praying to God, they quickly turned him over. Daniel was then thrown into the lions' den. However, God kept Daniel safe. He protected him. He shut the mouths of the lions and delivered Daniel. When the king came back the next day, he found Daniel safe amongst the lions. King Darius then commanded all the people in the kingdom to worship Daniel's God.

Daniel entered Babylon as a captive but because he faithfully sought-after God and His righteousness, he was rewarded. If we would seek the kingdom of God, if we would acknowledge, seek, and quench our daily hunger and thirst for righteousness, we will be filled. God says in 2 Chronicles 7:14 if my people who are called by my name will humble themselves and pray and seek my face and turn from their wicked ways, then I will hear from heaven and will forgive their sin and heal their land. We must seek after his righteousness continually.

In Matthew 7:7, Jesus says "ask and it will be given to you; seek and you will find; knock and the door will be opened to you." We have to keep asking, keep seeking, and keep knocking. No one else can fill the void you acknowledged by being poor in spirit. There is no job, no spouse or friend, and no amount of money that can satisfy the void. Blessed are those who hunger and thirst after righteousness, for they shall be filled.

In verse 7, Jesus states "Blessed are the merciful for they shall obtain mercy." This verse is about how we treat others. We are to show mercy to one another and forgive one another. In Matthew 18, Jesus tells a parable about a king who was settling accounts. One man was brought to him that owed him ten thousand talents, a currency used in that region and time, but he was unable to pay. Therefore, it was commanded that he and his family and all he had would be sold to pay off the debt. But the servant fell down before the king and asked for patience, as he would try to repay the debt. The king was moved with compassion, released him and forgave the debt completely.

Once the servant was forgiven, he immediately went and found a fellow servant that owed him a small amount of money. He laid hands on him, and not in a good way. Despite his fellow servant's request for mercy, he had him thrown into prison. When the king heard of this, he was angry. He had the servant brought before him. Due to his lack of compassion, due to his lack of mercy, the king had him delivered to the torturers. Jesus spoke to the crowd and said, "My father will do the same to you if you do not forgive one another."

God is a merciful god; and He is our example. We must have compassion for others, help others, and help to guide sinners to the salvation found in Jesus' love. The Lord's prayer states, "forgive us our trespasses, as we forgive those who trespass against us." By forgiving, you are accepting the reality of what has transpired; and through Jesus Christ, you find a way to live in a state of resolution with it.

Through forgiveness we shift our perspective from the things we are unable to change to the growth we can obtain from the situation. We learn from the situation; and we move forward.

There is a song my father sings entitled "Through It All" by Andrae Crouch. There's a verse in the song that says "I thank God for the mountains, and I thank Him for the valleys. I thank Him for the storms He brought me through. For if I'd never had a problem, I wouldn't know that God could solve them, I'd never know what faith in God could do." Then the chorus of the song comes in to say "Through it all, through it all, I've learned to trust in Jesus, I've learned to trust in God. Through it all, through it all, I've learned to depend upon His Word."

As I reflect on my journey, and all the mountains and all the valleys, I can truly say that through it all I have learned that I can trust Jesus. I have learned that I can stand on His word. I can have mercy, because I realize that God uses everything in my life to pave the path, I need to lead me to my destiny. As Paul states in Romans 8:28, "And we know that all things work together for good to those who love God, to those who are the called according to His purpose." Blessed are the merciful for they shall obtain mercy.

In verse 8, Jesus says "Blessed are the pure in heart for they shall see God."

David speaks of the testing of the heart in Psalms 17:3 when he says "You have tested my heart. You have tried me by fire." The purity of our heart is often shown in the midst of the fire. Revisiting the events in Daniel 3, there were three Hebrew boys Shadrach, Meshach, and Abednego who were promoted along with Daniel to positions in government. Jealousy grew among the advisors. But after conquering Jerusalem, King Nebuchadnezzar had a statue of himself built. He declared that all officials must worship this statue when the trumpet sounds, or they will be thrown into a fiery furnace. But the three Hebrew boys were pure in heart. Despite the consequence, their hearts belonged to God. When brought before the king they declared "The God we serve can save us from anything, including fire. But even if he does not, we will never worship an idol." This infuriated the king, and he ordered the fire to be heated seven times hotter than usual. But their hearts remained pure even when the heat of the situation turned up. They bound the boys up and threw them into the raging fire. But when the king looks into the furnace, he doesn't just see the three Hebrew boys. But he sees four people and the fourth one looked like the son of God. Stay pure in your heart, and you will see and experience God in the midst of the fire. Bless are the pure in heart for they shall see God.

Verse 9 states "Blessed are the peacemakers for they shall be called the children of God." There is a difference between being a peacekeeper and being a peacemaker. Peacekeepers will compromise and overlook wrongdoing just to keep the peace. However, peacemakers do not settle for fake peace, or a false perception of peace. Peacemakers seek to ensure that true peace is obtained so that the Prince of Peace can abide.

In Matthew 21, Jesus arrives at the temple in Jerusalem only to find that the temple had been turned into a shopping center. They were buying and selling all types of goods and services. Jesus kicked out those who were participating in the exploitation; and He turned over the tables and seats. Jesus then declared "it is written that my house shall be called a house of prayer, but you have turned it into a den of thieves." After this happened, the blind and lame were brought to him in the temple; and he healed them.

In order for miracles to transpire, we have to clean our house. This means sometimes we have to overturn some tables. We cannot keep allowing sin to fester and pretend like everything is okay. We must stand and declare as Jesus did "My house shall be a house of prayer." And just to ensure it's clear, who you will be praying to in this house of prayer, you can declare as Joshua did in Joshua 24, "As for me and my house, we will serve the Lord."

We also must realize that this is not just about external peace. This is also about internal peace. Once we recognize that our mind is cluttered and we are not obtaining the outcomes we need in life, we need to turn some tables over and deal with what is within our minds. Our thoughts must be examined and controlled. As Paul taught the church in Corinth, we need to bring "every thought into captivity to the obedience of Christ." We must make real peace, internally and externally by submitting to the Prince of Peace and obeying him. Blessed are the peacemakers for they shall be called the children of God.

In verse 10, Jesus says "Blessed are those who are persecuted for righteousness' sake, for theirs is the kingdom of heaven." Blessed and persecuted do not seem to fit very well together. But again, being blessed has nothing to do with your current situation or circumstance; it is about what you have access to.

In Acts 16, Paul and Silas casted out a spirit from a girl, who was a slave. Her masters were very upset that they could no longer profit off of her. So, they took Paul and Silas to the authorities. They then had Paul and Silas beaten and thrown into prison. The jailer was given specific instructions to ensure Paul and Silas did not escape. Paul and Silas were bound and tortured and placed in the innermost part of the prison. Although they were bound, they were still blessed. They were blessed because they had access to a power that would shake the very foundation of the institution that tried to keep them captive.

In the midnight hour, Paul and Silas prayed and worshipped God until a shaking began to happen. It was not just a shaking of their cell. But the foundation was shaken, and all those that were bound were now loosed. We should do as Paul and Silas did, and praise God in the midst of our persecution. We should praise Him regardless of our situation or circumstance.

Though Paul and Silas were bound, they still praised God. What does the praise of a bound man sound like? It is the sound of one recognizing who God is and what He is able to do. It goes beyond the current situation or circumstance. It spans the breadth of all the God has done, all that God has been, and all that He is. It is a statement of faith to God, showing that our praise is not conditional.

An unconditional praise is a demonstration; showing that whether I am in the prison cell like Paul, in the fire like the Hebrew boys, or facing the lions like Daniel, I will still praise you God! We cannot allow anything to cause us to forget what He's done for us. I do not have to be forced to praise God.

All I have to do is think about the goodness of Jesus and all that He has done for me. All I have to do is recall the times He healed my body. All I need to do is reflect on the many ways He has made for me, and my hands will go up, my feet will start jumping and my voice will cry out "Hallelujah!" Trials and tribulations cannot stop my praise! Disappointment cannot stop my praise! Discrimination cannot stop my praise. This is my story. This is my song; I am praising my savior all day long.

We need to trust and believe Him. We need to recognize that we need God. We need to acknowledge our wrongdoing and repent of our sins. We need to become meek and submit to God's will. We need to continuously seek His righteousness. We need to be merciful to others. We need to have a pure heart. We need to make peace. We need to praise Him in the midst of our persecution. If we do these things, we will be blessed. We would be able to access the favor, power, and spiritual joy we need to overcome.

Nutrient 4- Mercy

The Intention of This Nutrient:

We all have sinned. The realization of sin can lead one into a valley of guilt and shame. There are seasons in our life where we may engage in actions, habits, and behaviors that are costly to us and to others. However, God's mercy is a powerful gift that enables us to climb out of the valley of despair.

The first time we took our daughter bowling for the first time, we realized that she was not yet strong enough to have the necessary control to keep the ball in the center of the lane. Our daughter watched her first few rolls of the bowling ball go into the gutter, resulting in a score of zero on the scoreboard. She began to feel sad and frustrated as others' scores were increasing; but her score remained zero. We then added the bumpers to the lane, which serve as guardrails. The bumpers made the gutters no longer accessible. When the bowling ball came close to the gutter, the bumpers did not let the ball go into the gutter. The bumpers bounced the ball back to the center of the lane.

Similarly, the mercy that comes from Jesus' forgiveness of our sins makes the gutter no longer accessible. Once we confess our sins and truly repent, Jesus forgives our sins. He is able to save us from our sin. He is able to save us from the gutter. He is able to put us back in the center of the lane. He will facilitate our ability to increase our score on the board. In our own strength we may not have the necessary control to stay in the center lane, but with God's forgiveness, strength and power we can begin to move in the right direction to get the outcomes God has in store for us.

The purpose of this nutrient of mercy is to provide the humility and appreciation that comes from acknowledging our original sinful state and the mercy God provides. Through this nutrient we gain the assurance that God loves us and will equip us with the ability to live in a state where the gutter is no longer accessible. There is a limit to how far we have to go before we access the mercy of God to bring us back to where we need to be.

Repentance

Foundational Scripture

Psalms 51:1-19. Have mercy upon me, O God, According to Your lovingkindness; According to the multitude of Your tender mercies, Blot out my transgressions. [2] Wash me thoroughly from my iniquity, And

cleanse me from my sin. 3 For I
acknowledge my transgressions, and
my sin is always before me. 4 Against
You, You only, have I sinned, and
done this evil in Your sight— That
You may be found just when You
speak, and blameless when You judge.
5 Behold, I was brought forth in
iniquity, and in sin my mother
conceived me. 6 Behold, You desire
truth in the inward parts, and in the
hidden part You will make me to know
wisdom. 7 Purge me with hyssop, and I
shall be clean; Wash me, and I shall
be whiter than snow. 8 Make me hear
joy and gladness, That the bones You
have broken may rejoice. 9 Hide Your
face from my sins and blot out all my
iniquities. 10 Create in me a clean heart,
O God, and renew a steadfast spirit
within me. 11 Do not cast me away
from Your presence, and do not take
Your Holy Spirit from me. 12 Restore
to me the joy of Your salvation,
And uphold me by Your generous
Spirit. 13 Then I will teach transgressors

Your ways, and sinners shall be
converted to You. 14 Deliver me from
the guilt of bloodshed, O God, The
God of my salvation, and my tongue
shall sing aloud of Your righteousness.
15 O Lord, open my lips, and my mouth
shall show forth Your praise.
16 For You do not desire sacrifice, or
else I would give it; You do not delight
in burnt offering. 17 The sacrifices of
God are a broken spirit, A broken and
a contrite heart— These, O God, You
will not despise. 18 Do good in Your
good pleasure to Zion; Build the walls
of Jerusalem. 19 Then You shall be
pleased with the sacrifices of
righteousness, with burnt offering and
whole burnt offering; Then they shall
offer bulls on Your altar.

At some point in life, we will recognize a need for change. Romans 3:23 states "For all have sinned and fallen short of the glory of God." We have all sinned. We have all done wrong. Later in Romans it shows what outcomes we will receive if we do not change. For Romans 6:23 says "for the wages of sin is death, but the gift of God is eternal life." In Psalms 51, David cries out to God after he had sinned. David had an affair with a married woman named Bathsheba. He then schemed to have her husband killed. He recognized that the spiritual, mental and emotional place in which he was currently in was not where he wanted or needed to be. The wages of sin is death. David recognized where he was headed, and he wanted a change. He then cries out to God, as detailed in Psalms 51.

In verse 1 and 2, David asks God to blot out his transgressions and to wash away his iniquity. In Isaiah 43:25 it states, "I, even I, am He that blots out your transgressions for My own sake; And I will not remember your sins." In Psalms 32:1 David says, "Blessed is he whose transgression is forgiven, whose sin is covered." David did not want forgiveness as man forgives. Man says, “I will forgive but I will not forget.” But God offers true forgiveness for true repentance. God says He will blot out the sin and will not remember it. The sin is covered with the blood of the lamb.

In verse 3 and 4, David acknowledges his sin. David had committed adultery and murder. He grew tired of trying to cover up and disguise his sin. Although we know that all have sinned, we must acknowledge our sin. In Psalms 32:5, David states, "I acknowledged my sin to you, and my iniquity I have not hidden. I said, I will confess my transgressions to the Lord. And you forgave my sin." We cannot ignore our sin. We must confess it. For we have sinned against God, the one who created us, the one whose tender mercies wake us up each morning, the one who gave His son to die for us. David realized the magnitude of this and recognized that God is just and sovereign.

In verse 5 and 6, David notes that he was born into sin. However, he does not use this as an excuse. He is not satisfied with the sinful state he was born into. The life of a sinner is full of guilt, confusion, fear, frustration, failure, sadness, shame, and emptiness. David longed to be restored to the life of righteousness he once lived. He longed to return to that spiritual place he once was where he stated, "The Lord is my shepherd I shall not want."

In verse 7, David lets God know that he does not want an appearance or a form of godliness, he wants the real thing. He tells the Lord to purge him. He did not want a surface cleansing, so that people around him would think that he is free. But he wanted to be purged so that he will truly be free. As the word of God says, "Whom the Son sets free is truly free indeed."

In verse 8, David realizes that he will be punished, but he asked that his joy be restored after his punishment. He is willing to endure the punishment for his sin. He understands that "no sin will go unpunished." But he also realizes that God is a merciful and loving God, and that God would not put more on us than we can bear. Therefore, he knew that God would be there in the midst of his punishment. He knew that after his punishment God would restore his joy. For weeping may endure for a night, but joy comes in the morning. He knew that joy was coming.

In verse 10, David asks God for a clean heart. He wants to be renewed. He no longer wanted his old heart. For his old heart led him to adultery. He no longer wanted his old mind, for his old mind led him to try and cover up his adultery with murder. He wanted a clean heart, a clean mind, and a clean spirit. David was not satisfied with a life of sin. He wanted more. God wants more for us. Simple tweaks and small fixes would not do. David cried out to God asking God to give him a clean heart.

In verse 11 he says, don't cast me away. He still longs to be used. David knew he had sinned. But he had started a great work for God's glory, and he wanted to complete the work he had started. He did not want his sin to keep him from accomplishing the task he was commissioned to do. So, he wanted God to know that he was still able, willing, and available to do works for God's glory.

In verses 12 and 13, David requests joy in the midst of his current state of guilt and remorse. He understands that God has the power to grant joy in the darkest of moments. The type of joy that David is asking for is the joy Peter is referencing in 1 Peter 1:8 when he references the "joy unspeakable and full of glory." This is joy that cannot be expressed. Joy that can exist in the valley of regret, is inexpressible. It cannot be explained and is difficult to understand. This is because God's ways are higher than our ways his thoughts are higher than our thoughts. David recognizes the witness that will come from this unspeakable joy. He acknowledges that this is a joy that when other sinners see it, it will draw them to God.

In verses 14 and 15, David designates God as his savior. He makes his request known. David is calling out to his savior specifically asking to be saved from the guilt of the actions he took – the adultery, the murder, the sin. And David says that he will praise God and sing of His righteousness.

David uses verse 16 to declare his willingness to do what it would take to gain atonement to God. In verse 17 and 18, David gives God what he has. At this point, what David has to offer is a broken spirit, and a broken and repentant heart.

In verse 19, David speaks of his commitment to righteousness. Once we repent, we must become dedicated in our walk of righteousness. We must immediately get back on the right track. But we can't get on the right track and stand still. We must also progress. Once we have truly repented and turned back to God, He will forgive us. We must then walk in victory. We must get back on the right track and progress in triumph.

There is a hymn of the church titled “Love Lifted Me.” The first verse of the song says “I was sinking deep in sin, far from the peaceful shore. Very deeply stained within sinking to rise no more.” The song is speaking of that place when you feel far away from peace. You can feel like you are drowning in tears, drowning in heartache and pain, buried by burdens, stained with bitterness and depression. You can feel you are at the bottom with no hope and overcome with guilt and shame. When you get that low it is hard for others to reach to you. Parents cannot reach you; friends cannot reach you. But there is a master of the sea that will reach down with His nail-scarred hand. And from the water, He will lift you. He will remind you that He holds your future. And your life is worth the living just because He lives. The Lord is my refuge and my fortress in Him will I trust.

It may not be you in this situation of despair. It may be someone you love that is sinking in sin. You may have tried all you can to reach them, but they seem to be just beyond your reach. Your money cannot reach them. Your good advice cannot reach them. But do not give up on them. Turn them over to the Master of the sea. From the water of sadness, confusion, and pain, He is able to lift them to safety. His reach extends much further than our reach. None of us are ever too far that He is unable to reach us and pull us to safety and to peace.

Prayer for Forgiveness and Healing

In 2 Chronicles 7, God says "if My people who are called by My name will humble themselves, and pray and seek My face, and turn from their wicked ways, then I will hear from heaven, and will forgive their sin and heal their land."

In this scripture, God is speaking to Solomon. This is an answer to a prayer. In 2 Chronicles 6, Solomon is praying to God during the dedication of the Temple. Solomon had just finished building the temple for God, and the Lord's presence descended and filled the temple. Things seemed to be going well. But Solomon was the wisest man to live. He knew that although the saints were happy, and they were focused on God at that moment; he knew they could fall into sin in the next moment. Recognizing that, Solomon wanted to ensure that this temple, the house that was dedicated to God was a place where God would dwell, place where God would speak, a place where God would respond. This was Solomon's prayer; and in chapter 7, God showed up and spoke to Solomon. He answered his prayer.

Sometimes we can feel that no one hears us when we cry. No one cares when we are in need. We can feel as if no one sees us when we are hurting. But God cares, and He loves you. He hears you. He sees you; and He will answer. He will respond. God will take care of you! If you call on Him and trust Him, He will respond.

God's answer to Solomon's prayer was an answer consisting of an IF and a THEN statement. The IF part is up to us as we have a part to play. The THEN part is what God will do. God's answer to Solomon's prayer was: *IF* my people, who are called by My name will humble themselves, and pray and seek My face, and turn from their wicked ways, *THEN* I will hear from heaven, forgive their sin and heal their land.

God starts His answer by making it clear who He is talking about - He said if MY people who are called by MY name.

My People

We must have an intimate relationship with God; a deep relationship that goes beyond the surface. As Paul says in Romans 8, 'nothing can separate us from the love of God'. We cannot allow anything or anyone to pull us away from God!

Called by My Name

In John 10, Jesus says "My sheep know my voice." Can you hear Him when He calls? We get to know His voice by consistently reading the word and meditating on it. When you read the word, you begin to understand how God talks. You will notice the types of things He says. The call of the world changes constantly. But God is the same yesterday, today, and forevermore.

Humble Themselves

Once we have identified that we are His people who are called by his name, we must now assess our attitude and posture. We are to humble ourselves. We need to know who we are and who God is. In Romans 12 Paul says we should not think of ourselves more highly than we ought to think. When we think too much of ourselves, we begin to think we can handle everything ourselves;

and we cannot. Life is full of situations that we cannot handle. Life is full of circumstances, in which we do not have the answers. Life also has many situations we cannot fix. The pressure is too strong; and the burden is too heavy. Therefore, we must submit ourselves to the Almighty and all-powerful God - the one who is able to heal, to deliver, and to save.

Pray

We submit ourselves through prayer. Knowing that we cannot handle this on our own, we must cry out to God. At times, we cry out to the wrong people. We cry out to those who cannot help us. We cry out to those who talk about us and tell all our business. But with all that we may be going through right now, in the midst of fear, frustration, loneliness, hurt, and pain, we need to cry out to God. We need to cry out, just as it says in the hymn: "Father, I stretch my hands to Thee, no other help I know." When we do so, in faith, God will respond.

Seek My Face

Our next step is to seek His face. We must spend time learning about Him. Once we learn about Him, we will naturally seek Him. We will develop a hunger for the peace, joy, and happiness that He provides. Jesus tells us in Matthew 6 "Seek ye first the kingdom of God and His righteousness, and all these things shall be added unto you."

There is a level of faith that comes with seeking. When you need it bad enough, you keep seeking. You don't give up on it. If you have to pray more than once, you keep seeking. If you have to fast for it, you keep seeking. You keep seeking because it means that much. Once we get a little taste of Jesus, once we taste and see that he is good, once we truly try him and find that He is the answer; we will seek after Him. We will seek after His guidance and His instruction. I am not talking about what someone told you about Him, I'm talking about when you truly taste and see Him for yourself. That's when you become fully persuaded. That's when you can stand firm and say, "you can't make me doubt Him because I know too much about Him." I've tasted of His mercy and His grace. I have tasted His love and care. And I now seek after Him more and more.

Turn From our Wicked Ways

And when we are seeking after Him, we will then turn from the things that pull us away from Him. We must turn our backs on sin. It is not enough to ask for forgiveness, if we are still engaging in the same sins. We have to turn away and move in a different direction. Paul said in Philippians 3, "This one thing I do, forgetting those things which are behind, and I press towards those things which are ahead." This is a new day. We can turn from the things which are behind us. We can turn from our sin and guilt. We can turn from our past. We do not have to live under the limitations of our past. We are new creatures. Turn your back from what once was; and turn your face to God and towards what will be, through Him. God said, "Behold I am doing a new thing and it shall now spring forth."

He is faithful. If He said it, He will do it. We do our part, and He will do His. I am a witness. For I came to Jesus just as I was, weary, worn, and sad, and I found in Him a resting place and He has made me glad. He made me glad because He heard me, He forgave me, and He healed me. Thank you, Jesus.

Change your perspective and attitude by humbling yourself. Cry out to God in prayer. Seek God and His righteousness. As you seek His righteousness, turn away from anything that pulls you away from God. When we do, God will hear, forgive and heal us! Let the healing begin!

Restoration

Foundational Scripture

Luke 13: 10-13. Now He was
teaching in one of the synagogues on
the Sabbath. [11] And behold, there was
a woman who had a spirit of infirmity
eighteen years, and was bent over and
could in no way raise herself up. [12] But
when Jesus saw her, He called her to
Him and said to her, "Woman, you
are loosed from your infirmity."
[13] And He laid His hands on her, and
immediately she was made straight,
and glorified God.

Jesus tells us in John 16:33 "In this life

you will have tribulations." Peter tells us in 1 Peter 4, "Beloved do not think it strange concerning the fiery trial which is to try you." We are in spiritual warfare constantly, and there our times where we are spiritually drained. There may be times where we can wake up in the morning at 8:00, and by 8:15, we are exhausted. When we go through the fires and trials of this life, we need God to restore us.

Jesus tells us in John 10, that Satan comes to steal, kill and destroy. But Jesus said that he comes that we might have life, and that we might have it more abundantly. So even when you've been thorough battles that have stolen your joy, killed your dreams and destroyed your self-esteem, it is not over. Paul tells us in Philippians 1 "He who began a good work in you will complete it." He will not give up on you, regardless of what you may have done. It is not over until you are restored and living abundantly.

When you feel guilty and lost and as though you are drowning in darkness and despair, please know that you do not have to stay there. His love can reach you in the lowest and darkest places. It does not matter how long you have been there.

In Luke 13 Jesus was teaching in the synagogue on the Sabbath. There was a woman who had a spirit of infirmity for 18 years. She was bent over and could not raise herself up. But when Jesus saw her, He called her to Him and said, "Woman you are loosed from your infirmity." He laid hands on her, and she was immediately able to stand up straight and she glorified God. For 18 years, she had been stuck in the same position with the same limited view. She had tried to raise herself up and could not.

We often try to elevate ourselves restore our own mind, revive our own hopes; but we cannot. David tells us in Psalm 23, He restores my soul. As mentioned in the Power to Resurrect section, in John 11, Lazarus had died. The tomb where Lazarus was buried had a stone blocking the entrance. When Jesus asked that the stone be rolled away, Lazarus' sister Martha was concerned with the potential smell.

At times, we try to hide our brokenness. We must not hide behind stones of shame and guilt, substances or relationships. Lazarus' sister told Jesus not to move the stone. There are times when those around us may want to keep the stone in place and may not want the world to smell the stench of our sin and brokenness. But Paul says in Romans 8, "for I reckon that the suffering of this present time is not worthy to be compared to the glory that shall be revealed in us." Do not allow someone else's pride to keep you from salvation and restoration. Take the stone away. You can say "Lord I am tired of hiding my pain and my brokenness. I am now exposing them to you. This is who I am and where I am. I am giving it all to you so that you can truly make me whole."

Jesus said to Martha Did I not tell you that if you would believe you would see the glory of God? You have to believe that Jesus can and will restore you. If you will cry out to Him in truth and believe that He can restore you, He will. Jesus understands; for He also needed restoration.

In Matthew 26, Jesus was in the Garden at Gethsemane. Scripture says that Jesus was sorrowful and distressed. Jesus asked his disciples to stay with him while he prayed. He then went a little farther and prayed. He cried out to God "Father if it is possible let this cup pass from me. Nevertheless, not my will but thine will be done." Jesus went through much pain and anguish on His way to the cross. He was crucified, died and was buried. But that's not the end of the story. His life was restored. He rose with all power in His hands.

Paul said in 2 Corinthians 4 "He who raised up the Lord Jesus will also raise us up." We do not know what tomorrow will bring; but because He lives, we can face it. Because He lives, we can make it. No matter what you have been through, no matter what you have done, my life and your life is worth the living just because He lives.

He restores us for a purpose. There has to be something on the other side of this storm. It hurt too bad for there to not be any gain. The pain was too deep for there to be no progress. You will gain far more in your future, than you lost in your past. Because when Jesus restores you, He doesn't just bring you back to where you were, but He increases your capacity. You now know Him on a deeper level. He will take you higher than you ever dreamed.

Forgiveness

God commissions us to forgive others. In Matthew 6:14-15 it states, "For if you forgive men their trespasses, your heavenly Father will also forgive you. But if you do not forgive men their trespasses, neither will your Father forgive your trespasses." In Matthew 5:7, says, "blessed are the merciful, for they shall obtain mercy." Since we have had our sins forgiven, we must forgive the sins of others.

Jesus had endured much persecution before He was nailed to the cross. One of His followers, Judas Iscariot, had betrayed Him. One of His closest followers, Peter, denies Him. Matthew 27:15-55 details the persecution Jesus endures. Jesus stood before a multitude, many of which had witnessed the very work of God through Jesus' miracle. The multitude chose to set a notorious prisoner, Barabbas, free instead of setting Jesus free. Jesus listened as the multitude shouted their desire for his fate, "Crucify Him, Crucify Him." The soldiers then took Jesus away and the entire military force gathered around Him. They stripped His clothes and put a scarlet robe on Him. They made a crown of thorns and placed it on His head. They mocked Him. They spat in His face. They beat Him in the head with a stick. They then took Him to be crucified.

They placed nails in His hands and feet and hung Him on the cross. All the while, the foolish crowd mocked Him, daring Him to come down from the cross. One of the thieves that hung beside Him said to Jesus, "If you are truly the Son of God, save yourself and us too." But in the midst of all this persecution, oppression, and injustice, Jesus looks to heaven and states in

Luke 23:34, "Father, forgive them, for they do not know what they do."

As Jesus was praying to God to forgive His persecutors, they were dividing His clothes. Jesus was able to forgive in the midst of His mistreatment. We tend to wait for the injustice to subside. We tend to wait until those who have wronged us have learned their lesson. But Jesus asked God to forgive them while they were performing this great injustice. Little did the thief that taunted Jesus know, that Jesus still had the power to save himself and them. Little did the multitude know, that He had the power to strike all of them. But Jesus' love for us is immeasurable. Jesus' dedication to fulfilling the will of God is undeniable.

In the face of persecution, when most of us fold, Jesus prevailed. The foolish crowd was taunting Him, saying they would believe if He came down. However, they did not realize that if

He had come down from the cross, their belief would not be enough. For there would be no way back to God. If He had come down from the cross, our fate would have been sealed. We would have been born into sin and died in sin. How foolish our complaining is when we do not know the will of God.

It is easy to say, "Well this is Jesus, I am only human, I cannot have that amount of forgiveness and love." However, the word of God refutes that. In Acts 7:60 Stephen demonstrated the same type of forgiving spirit. As Stephen was being stoned to death he cries out to God, "Lord, do not charge them with this sin." When many of us would have cried out, "Lord charge them double for this sin," Stephen showed that Christ-like love and forgiveness and asked that God forgive those who were killing him.

No More Stones

Foundational Scripture
John 8:1-11. But Jesus went to the
Mount of Olives. [2] Now early in the
morning He came again into the
temple, and all the people came to
Him; and He sat down and taught
them. [3] Then the scribes and Pharisees
brought to Him a woman caught in
adultery. And when they had set her
in the midst, [4] they said to Him,
"Teacher, this woman was caught
in adultery, in the very act. [5] Now
Moses, in the law, commanded us that
such should be stoned. But what do
You say" [6] This they said, testing
Him, that they might have something
of which to accuse Him. But Jesus
stooped down and wrote on the
ground with His finger, as though He
did not hear. [7] So when they continued
asking Him, He raised Himself up and
said to them, "He who is without sin
among you, let him throw a stone at
her first." [8] And again He stooped

down and wrote on the ground. [9] Then
those who heard it, being convicted
by their conscience, went out one by
one, beginning with the oldest even to
the last. And Jesus was left alone, and
the woman standing in the midst.
[10] When Jesus had raised Himself
up and saw no one but the woman, He
said to her, "Woman, where are those
accusers of yours? Has no one
condemned you?" [11] She said, "No
one, Lord." And Jesus said to
her, "Neither do I condemn you;
go and sin no more."

In John 8:1-11, the scribes and Pharisees bought an adulterous woman to Jesus. They said they had caught her in the very act. They informed Jesus that the Law of Moses says that one accused of adultery should be stoned to death. In verse 7 Jesus responds to them by saying, "He who is without sin among you, let him throw the first stone." As written in the Bible, "All have sinned and fallen short of the glory of God." Therefore, that first stone will never be thrown. We have no right to throw stones, or insults, or judgment. Therefore, since we have been forgiven, let us forgive others. Let us not allow pride to get in the way of us doing what God commissions us to do. We must forgive one another. For "blessed is the merciful, for they shall obtain mercy."

Salvation

Life is not easy. There are trials and tribulations that we will all face. No one will go through life without enduring any problems. Even Jesus, free of sin, had to endure trials.

It is up to us whether we endure these trials alone; or whether we endure our trials with a savior who is all-powerful and will fight our battles for us. We will all face storms in life. But facing the storm is much easier when you are able to call on the Prince of Peace who can speak to the storm in your life and cause it to subside. It is a difference between facing an infirmity in the body alone with no one to rely on and being able to call on the one who stated in Exodus 15:26, "I am the God that heals you." We will encounter financial difficulties. But it is much easier to overcome those difficulties when you know Jehovah Jireh, who is your provider. No one can fight the battle of life alone. The choice is whether to attempt to fight it alone and surely fail; or to walk the journey of life with the savior who has already won the victory.

Jesus is the only one that can save us from our sins. The Bible is descriptive when describing the life and fate of sinners. Romans 6:23 states, "For the wages of sin is death, but the gift of God is eternal life in Christ Jesus our Lord." Therefore, if a sinner does not repent and follow Christ, the one true way to God, he will have to pay the wages of his sin. However, once a sinner repents and comes to Christ, he will not have to pay this wage. For Christ paid the wage for the repented heart on the cross.

John 3:16 states, "For God so loved the world that He gave His only begotten Son, that whoever believes in Him should not perish but have everlasting life." We will all die the first death. But our choice between a life of sin or salvation will determine our fate after the first death. Do we choose eternal life in heaven with God, or do we choose to burn eternally in the lake of fire?

It seems to be an obvious choice; it seems to be a no-brainer. However, there are millions of sinners who have yet to make the choice to follow God. There are millions who are still fighting the battle of life on their own. They are fighting a losing battle. 1 Corinthians 1:18 states, "For the message of the cross is foolishness to those who are perishing, but to us who are being saved it is the power of God." Those who choose to not believe are perishing.

Isaiah 59:2 says, "But your iniquities have separated you from your God; and your sins have hidden His face from you, so that He will not hear." Life without God offers no relief and no deliverance. It is utter darkness and emptiness. Ephesians 2:12 describes life without God as follows, "that at that time you were without Christ, being aliens from the commonwealth of Israel and strangers from the covenants of promise, having no hope and without God in the world." Without God, we are a free target for Satan. We have no protection against the devil. And as 1 Peter 5:8 states, "your adversary the devil walks about like a roaring lion, seeking whom he may devour."

Proverbs 13:21-22 describes the life of sinners as follows, "Evil pursues sinners, but to the righteous, good shall be repaid. A good man leaves an inheritance to his children's children, but the wealth of the sinner is stored up for the righteous." Haggai 1:6 states, "You have sown much, and bring in little; you eat, but do not have enough; you drink, but you are not filled with drink; you clothe yourselves, but no one is warm; And he who earns wages, earns wages to put into a bag with holes." What a frustrating way to live!

Have you ever found that you earn money, but it seems to disappear faster than it comes? Have you ever found that you do all you can to save and keep yourself afloat; but you seem to always be behind? If so, you must ask yourself, "Have I truly repented?" If so, ask yourself, "Am I living a life rooted in the principles within the word of God? Am I bringing my tithes and offerings into the storehouse?" In order to abandon this frustrating life of working and struggling, trying and failing, sacrificing and losing; we must give our whole life to Christ.

That way, we can triumph over our trials and tribulations. We can have joy in the knowledge that as the Bible says in Psalms 30:5, "For His anger is but for a moment, His favor is for life; Weeping may endure for a night, but joy comes in the morning." We can live our life knowing that no matter what the situation may look like, the word of God says in Romans 8:28, "And we know that all things work together for good to those who love God, to those who are the called according to His purpose."

Confess - The first step to salvation is to confess our sin. Simply state, "Lord, I know I am a sinner. I have done wrong. However, I do not wish to remain in this sinful state." God knows that we are born into sin. The Bible says in Romans 3:23, "for all have sinned and fall short of the glory of God." But Isaiah 43:25 states, "I, even I, am He who blots out your transgressions for My own sake; And I will not remember your sins." He will forgive your sins and will not hold them over your head. He will not treat us as man treats us. He will not expose and shame us by pulling "skeletons out of the closet." He will take those dry bones and revive them. He will take the gifts that you once used for evil; and He will teach you how to use them for His glory, that you may better serve him. As the song "It is Well with My Soul" states, "My sin oh the bliss of this glorious thought. My sin, not in part, but the whole, is nailed to the cross and I bear it no more. Praise the Lord! Praise the Lord, Oh my soul!"

Believe - The next step to salvation is to believe. Simply state, "God, I believe that you loved me so much that you gave your son to die on the cross for me. He paid the price for our sin. Then He arose on the third day as He had promised with all power in His hands. He is alive!"

Isaiah 53:5-6 states, "But He was wounded for our transgressions, He was bruised for our iniquities; The chastisement for our peace was upon Him, And by His stripes we are healed. All we like sheep have gone astray; We have turned, everyone, to his own way; And the Lord has laid on Him the iniquity of us all." Jesus was betrayed, denied, mocked, beaten, taunted, spat at, stripped, stabbed, laughed at and crucified all on our behalf, and on the behalf of those who were persecuting Him. He suffered this cruel and unjust death for you and me. We were the guilty ones; He had not committed any sin. You and I committed the crime; and Jesus paid the price.

All He asks is that we believe in Him. He has definitely proven Himself worthy of our belief and faith. John 1:12 states, "But as many as received Him, to them He gave the right to become children of God, to those who believe in His name." Once we believe, we are now children of God. Just as a father takes care of his children, so our heavenly father will care for us. The Bible says we are joint heirs with Jesus. We can access all the power Jesus has, as well. We are given an amazing opportunity, a wonderful gift, if we simply believe.

Let him in - The final step to salvation is to ask Jesus to come into your life and take control. Revelations 3:20 states, "Behold, I stand at the door and knock. If anyone hears My voice and opens the door, I will come in to him and dine with him, and he with Me." He is waiting for the invitation from us. No matter how far we have drifted, no matter how bad we think we are, He is our creator. He loves us. He wants us to be the person we were created to be.

He is more than able to transform our lives into a valuable gift that can be shared with others. He has already paid the price for us. All we have to do is give Him a chance. What do we have to lose? We have everything to gain. Allow Him to come in and transform your life; and began walking in victory today.

Choices

Over the course of a lifetime, there are certain lessons, which once learned, will carry us far down the road to becoming who God wants us to be. These lessons will help us live out God's plan for our lives. Many of these lessons will help us face specific situations we will meet along the way. Some lessons will simply help us get off to the right start and stay grounded and rooted in the teachings of God's word. Some lessons help us at very young ages; and some lessons assist us in growing, and in our adult lives. We will look at a range of situations during this learning cycle.

Stay Alert and Answer Strong

It is critical that we develop a trait of active listening and attentiveness. John 10:10 tells us that the devil, “The thief does not come except to steal, and to kill, and to destroy.” But Jesus then says, “I have come that they may have life, and that they may have *it* more abundantly.” We have to be alert and connected to God to ensure we are aware of the various spiritual battles that we may face. We must also develop the habit of giving strong and sure responses when presented with a choice to make.

In the following poem, "I Have a Choice” written in 2000 by my father, WJ Morris, multiple choices are outlined, and a response provided. As you read this poem, respond with your choice out loud in a very loud, strong, firm and decisive manner.

I HAVE A CHOICE

I HAVE A CHOICE !!!
I will praise the Lord
Both day and night;
Between right and wrong
I will choose RIGHT!

I HAVE A CHOICE !!!
The Lord will help me
Do the things that I should;
Between good and bad,
I will choose GOOD!

I HAVE A CHOICE !!!
I put all of my faith
In God of Heaven above;
Between love and hate,
I will choose LOVE!

I HAVE A CHOICE !!!
Jesus - no closer friend
Will ever you find;
Between kind and mean,
I will be KIND!

I HAVE A CHOICE !!!
From the bondage of sin,
It's the blood of the Lamb that frees us;
Between Jesus and the devil,
I CHOSE JESUS!!!!

-By WJ Morris

This poem provides an opportunity to reflect on the various choices and decisions we may face in life. When the enemy sends someone across your path with bad advice and wrong thinking, you must listen well to understand clearly what is being offered or asked. Then you must respond firmly with a strong decision to do the things that will please God. Above all, be determined that nothing can take away your ability to choose to please God; you have a choice to follow God!! Use your choice and use your voice!

Nutrient 5 – Grace

The Intention of This Nutrient: While mercy is forgiveness of our debt; grace is receiving benefits we do not deserve and have not earned. As we go through life, we may experience moments of goodness, surprising acts of kindness, or times of relief and joy. It is through the grace of God that we experience the evidential goodness of God.

As a child my son was fascinated by the automatic doors that would open when he would walk by them. At his age, he was not yet able to push or pull doors open. But with these doors, he doesn't have to push or pull he just has to stand in the right spot. That was amazing to him. It is also amazing to me when I reflect on the moments that doors opened for me when I didn't have to apply force to them. I just had to be standing in the right spot or moving in the right direction.

The intention of the grace nutrient is to demonstrate to goodness of God as He provides us with unmerited, undeserved favor. He looks beyond our faults, and He sees our needs and our wants. But He does not stop at seeing our needs. He meets our needs. Thank you, God, for your grace!

In order to grow in grace, we must first understand what grace is. Grace is defined as unmerited favor. Justice means you get what you deserve. Mercy means that you do not get what you deserve. The Bible says the wages of sin is death. But Jesus paid the price for us when he died on Calvary. Therefore, we have mercy and do not get what we deserve. For God so loved the world that He gave His only begotten son that whosoever believes in Him will not perish (through mercy); but will have everlasting life (through grace). The grace we receive, the unmerited, unearned favor comes in many forms. It comes in the form of blessings, abilities, and gifts. It can also be in the form of protection, endurance, strength, and peace. Grace is easy when things are going well. It's easy to walk in peace on payday. It's easy to have joy after receiving a miraculously good report from the doctor. But where we grow in grace are in the hard times, in those midnight hours, in those periods of pain, heartache, and hardship. That is where we grow in grace.

In John 16:33, Jesus says that in this life we will have trials. But He also says for us to be of good cheer for He has overcome the world. He overcame the world when He rose from the dead; and through that sacrifice, we have grace. Grace is also the vehicle that takes us from where we are to where God has called us to be. Paul says in 1 Corinthians 15:9-10 "For I am the least of the apostles who am not worthy to be called an apostle because I persecuted the church of God. I am what I am and his grace towards me was not in vain." It was God's grace that carried Paul from being Saul when he was persecuting the Christians to when God changed his name. He then became a mighty servant of God, started many churches, and wrote books of the Bible. It was through God's grace.

However, Paul had to go through many trials for which he had to rely on God's grace to get him through. In 2 Corinthians 12:7-10 Paul says "lest I should be exalted above measure by the abundance of the revelations, a thorn in the flesh was given to me, a messenger of Satan to buffet me, lest I be exalted above measure.

Concerning this thing I pleaded with the Lord three times that it might depart from me. And He said to me, "My grace is sufficient for you, for My strength is made perfect in weakness." Therefore, most gladly I will rather boast in my infirmities, that the power of Christ may rest upon me. Therefore, I take pleasure in infirmities, in reproaches, in needs, in persecutions, in distresses, for Christ's sake. For when I am weak, then I am strong."

The thorn that was in Paul's flesh caused him great pain and anguish. He asked God three times to remove it. There was a specific response he wanted from God. It reminds me of children's creative way of interpreting conversations. Children at times can feel that because they ask for something then it shall be done, especially if they asked nicely. This is an example of child-like faith. Where a child may ask to have something or to go somewhere. Regardless of the subsequent response, the next time the child discusses it, the conversation is recapped differently. It is recapped as "Remember you promised you were going to buy me something or take me somewhere." We often treat God the same way. We feel that just because we ask and especially if we throw some scriptures in our request, we expect it to be done. But God's will is sovereign.

When Paul made this request in 2 Corinthian 12: 8, he would have wanted God to respond to say, "Paul since you have been converted you have been a great servant and because of your faith I will remove this thorn." But that was not God's response. God's response was I am not going to remove this thorn, but my grace is sufficient. Before Jesus was taken to be crucified, he asked God to "remove the cup from him". He was asking God to remove the burden of the intended path of crucifixion from him. But Jesus then added "Not my will, thy will be done." Jesus recognized that though he may have asked for this cup to be removed, God's will is sovereign. And Jesus yielded to God's will.

No matter what the situation may be, we have to learn to bloom right where we are planted. We must learn to be content in whatever state we are in for we know God is in control. God has a purpose for your path. He has a purpose for every trial you will face. God has the power to heal and deliver; but He also has the power to give you grace to see you through the trial.

God is saying to us, "my grace is sufficient. My grace was sufficient to save you. My grace was sufficient to raise you; and my grace is sufficient to carry you through this storm." As you are going through the storm and once you come through the storm, you can declare as Paul said, "I am what I am because of God's grace." Because of God's grace I don't look like what I have been through. Because of God's grace I don't look like what I am going through right now. I praise God for the grace He provided to carry me through my storms.

Growing In Grace

Grace was first mentioned in the Bible to describe Noah. The scripture says that "Noah found grace in the eyes of the Lord." That grace that Noah found was accessed through faith & obedience. Through faith Noah obeyed God and despite all those that mocked him, despite all those who didn't understand him; he built the ark as God commanded to save him and his family.

In order for us to access God's grace, we must also exhibit faith and obedience. Ephesians 2:8 states "By grace are ye have been saved through faith." By faith we must do as Noah did and despite our doubters and our naysayers, we must listen to God's voice. We must build a structure for our lives by which we access grace and our saved. By faith, we must believe that Jesus is the son of God, that He came here on Earth and was born to a virgin named Mary. By faith, we must believe that He lived a life without sin or blemish. He died on the cross as a sacrifice for our sin. By faith, we must believe that He rose from the dead with all power in His hand. It is this sacrifice that provides the grace that allows us to be saved.

Grace comes at a price; and the price was the blood of Jesus. The blood of an undefiled sacrifice has always been a powerful element of salvation and atonement. When the Israelites were in Egypt, and the final plague was released, God instructed the Israelites to put the blood of an undefiled lamb around their door. God then said to them, 'When I see the blood, the plague will not be upon you to destroy you." When I see the blood, I will know you are protected. I will know you are mine. His blood must be visible in our lives.

When we are born into this world, we are born into sin. That sin has to be washed away. What can wash away my sin? The songwriter says, "Nothing but the blood of Jesus". Mohammed's blood cannot wash my sin away. You cannot get blood from a statute of Buddha to cleanse anyone. Nothing but the blood of Jesus will work. The songwriter goes on to say, "what can make me whole again?" No one on this Earth can make me whole. No job or social status can make me whole. Nothing but the blood of Jesus will work. Another songwriter writes about his blood and says, 'It reaches to the highest mountain." And just in case you are not on the mountaintop right now, the songwriter reminds us that it also "flows to the lowest valley." It is this blood that gives me strength from day to day. And this blood will never lose its power. The blood of our resurrected savior still works. It was shed over two thousand years ago, but it still works today. For I know it was the blood that saved me.

His grace saves. Salvation is not something God was obligated to provide. The Bible says that "the wages of sin is death." Since we have all sinned & fallen short of the glory of God, for justice to be served we should have died for our sin. We were guilty. According to the law of Moses, blood would have to be shed. The law of Moses instituted that blood sacrifice was required for the atonement of sin. But just as the verdict was being delivered, just as the sentence was being passed; God stepped in, and said wait a minute, by grace are ye saved.

John said, "We have all received grace for grace." God replaced the grace under the law of Moses with the grace and truth that came from Jesus' sacrifice on the cross. Whenever God replaces something, He always upgrades it. Whatever cross you are carrying right now, one day you will exchange it. That cross of sickness, that cross of loneliness, that cross of burdens, one day you will exchange it. In Romans 8:18 Paul states, "for I reckon that the sufferings of this present time are not worthy to be compared with the glory that shall be revealed in us." One day we will exchange these present sufferings for glory. We will exchange our trials for triumph, our burdens for blessings, our persecution for power, our disaster for deliverance. One day we will exchange it. This exchange is only made possible by grace.

Not only does His grace save us, but through His grace He cares for us, and

He will make us whole. If we take another look at Mark 4, when Jesus and His disciples were out at sea in a boat. Suddenly a mighty storm arose, and the waves begin to rise up and cover the boat. The boat began to fill with water. The disciples were scared. They looked around saw that Jesus was sleeping; and they panicked. They woke him up said “Master do you care that we are perishing?”

So often we go to Jesus and ask the same thing. “Lord do you see this storm in my life? Do you see all this pain I am enduring right now? Do you see all the burdens I am trying my best to carry? Did you hear that report I just got from the doctor? Did you see that final notice stamp on that bill? Do you care?” But Jesus is saying to us “Calm down, you have grace. I am still the Shepherd of your life. I do not have to fill out a request form and await an approval process. All I have to say is “peace”, all I have to say is “healed”, all I need to say is "delivered," and it shall be done. I have been given the name that is above every name, that at the name of Jesus every knee shall bows every tongue shall confess that he is Lord." At the name of Jesus, your sickness, your burdens, your trials must bow down.

The same Peter that was out at sea and was among the disciples that woke Jesus up to ask Him if He cared; provides some guidance in 1 Peter 5 when he says, "Cast your cares on Him because he cares for you". He's saying "I have tried Him for myself, and I have seen what He does when storms come out of nowhere. I have seen what He does in the midst of the storm. I have seen what He does when the waves rise up and overtake you. I have seen what He does when the wind is blowing so hard you can barely stand. Cast all your cares on Him for He cares for you."

Not only through His grace does He care for you; but He will make you whole. When we look again at Matthew 8, and we explore deeper into how Jesus performed the healing; we will see an example of Jesus' commitment to make us whole. In Matthew 8, the leper came towards Jesus and said, "Lord if you are willing you can make me clean." Jesus then reached out and touched Him, in the condition he was in. Jesus then said "I am willing. Be clean."

In biblical times, a leper was seen as a disgrace, unclean, and disgusting. Lepers were often quarantined and separated from the rest of the population. Leprosy was highly contagious. But Jesus did not heal this leper from afar; but He reached out and touched Him.

There are times in life where you can find yourself in situations or conditions that seem so dark, so hectic that others want nothing to do with you. No one wants to reach out and give you a "Sunday hug." No one wants to reach out and call you or visit you in the hospital. They do not know what to say; it is too much for them to handle. But we have a savior who cares. We have a savior that will reach out and touch you in the midst of what you are going through.

When others are turning their backs and walking out on you; He is running to you. He looks at you and says "my child needs to feel my touch of love right now. My child needs me to wrap my arms around them and say my child I love you. I am willing. I am willing to sit with you in the midnight hour when everyone else is fast asleep and you are tossing and turning with the burdens you are carrying. I am willing to sit with you on the job where you may be dealing with all types of disrespect and injustice. I am willing. Be clean, be whole, be set free by the grace of God." He looks beyond every one of our faults and sees and meets our needs.

Not only does He care, not only does His grace make us whole; but His grace also revives and delivers. Jesus was crucified and died for our sins. He was buried; but He did not stay buried. He rose from the dead with all power in His hands. Death could not defeat Him. The grave could not hold Him in the ground. Just as death could not defeat Him, we ourselves cannot be defeated.

Romans 6:5 says, "for if we have been planted together in the likeness of His death, we shall also be in the likeness of His resurrection." We shall not be defeated. All those buried dreams, hopes, joys that have been buried under negativity, doubt and insecurity shall rise by the grace of God. The enemy thought you were done. He thought you had given up. He thought he had put your future to death. But He did not realize that you were going to read this today and learn that God says in Jeremiah 29:11 "for I know the plans I have for you says the Lord. Plans for good and not for evil, to give you a future and a hope." And we can stand by grace and faith in the spirit of the resurrected king and declare "O death where is thy victory? O grave where is thy sting?"

Because we now have grace, we are more than conquerors through Him who loved us. Because we now have grace, we can do all things through Christ who strengthens us. Because we now have grace, we can be strong and courageous for the Lord our God is with us wherever we go. Because we now have grace, all the sin that we have committed has been nailed to the cross and we do not have to bear it anymore. Thank you, God, for your grace.

Because our sin has indeed been nailed to the cross, we can choose to release that sin and guilt; and choose to live in grace today. Jesus' sacrifice on the cross provided us with deliverance. But the enemy does not want us to know we have been delivered. The enemy wants to keep us bound. He does not want us to know that by grace we have been delivered. Jesus has prepared our way out. When Jesus was buried in the tomb, they put a guard at the entrance of the tomb. They wanted to ensure there was no way for anyone to come and carry Jesus' body out. But they had no control over what was going on inside of the tomb. They underestimated God's power.

At times, we can find ourselves in situations where we can feel trapped. It can seem as if every door of escape, every door of opportunity, has been locked and sealed. But do not worry about those closed doors. Let them close every single door; because I can hear my heavenly father say "who needs a door? I will open a window from heaven and pour you out a blessing you won't have room to receive." You cannot limit God's power.

There are times where we can find ourselves approaching a Red Sea as the Israelites did when they were leaving Egypt. They finally were delivered, and they get to the Red Sea. This would have been fine, except that the Egyptian army was steadily chasing and pressing them. There are times in life where we are finally progressing. We are finally moving forward; but then we hit a roadblock. The enemy knows we hit that roadblock. He knows we are trapped at the sea; and he is steadily pressing us.

You may have lost a job. But now, your car breaks down, appliances stop working, and bills start piling up. The enemy thinks he has you trapped. He can see the sea before you; and he knows you do not have a boat to float on. But I can hear my heavenly father say "who needs a boat? I will split this sea in half and prepare a path of praise for you to walk through". As David said, "yea though I walk through the valley of the shadow of death I will fear no evil for you are with me". And because you are with me oh God, I know that no weapon formed against me will prosper. A thousand may fall at my side, ten thousand at my right hand; but they shall not come near me.

I know firsthand about God's amazing grace. Amazing grace, how sweet the sound that saved a wretch like me. If you do not know how sweet His amazing grace is, it sounds like this. John 3:16 states for God so loved the world that He gave His only begotten son that whosoever believes in Him should not perish but shall have ever lasting life." That sounds sweet to me. Romans 6:23 says "for the wages of sin is death but the gift of God is eternal life." That's a sweet sound to me. John 10:10 states "The thief comes to steal, kill, and destroy." But Jesus said, I come that you might have life and that you may have it more abundantly." That sounds sweet to me. David says, "taste and see that the Lord is good."

Have you tried Him? Have you seen His grace at work in your life? I know what He's done for me so I must thank Him for his grace. For if no one else will praise God, I will praise God. If no one else can call God a healer, I can call God a healer. If no one else can call God a way maker, I can call Him a way maker. For in the day when I cried out to God, He answered me and made me bold with strength in my soul.

For I came to Jesus just as I was, weary, worn, sad; but I found something in Him. I found in Him a resting place, and He has made me glad. It is this gladness that arise with each and every day.

It is this gladness and gratefulness that I have when I approach His throne of grace. This is what enables me to enter His gates with thanksgiving and into His courts with praise. I praise God for His sacrifice on Calvary. I praise Jesus for shedding His blood to allow me access to God's grace. I praise God for saving me, for caring for me, for healing me, for reviving me, and for delivering me. Thank you, God, for your grace.

Nutrient 6- Purpose

The Intention of This Nutrient: There is a difference in simply existing and living with a purpose. At times, we can go through seasons where we realize that we are not living up to our full potential. We can feel as if we are floating through life with no direction or purpose. But God is our guide. He knows our purpose.

There is a children's movie entitled "The Lion King". In one scene of the movie, the father lion, named Mufasa, speaks to his son Simba. He says to him "look inside yourself. You are more than what you have become." The wisdom shared with Simba throughout the movie does not stop there. At another point in the movie, the baboon named Rafiki shares wisdom with Simba as well. Rafiki tells Simba "Oh yes the past can hurt.

But the way I see it, you can either run from it or learn from it." Both of these quotations speak to discovering and living in the purpose for which you are created. A caterpillar will never reach its intended heights and abilities until it becomes a butterfly. In our lives we must do more than exist. We must seek God's will for our lives. If we reflect on and unpack our journey, we will reveal themes that point us to our purpose. We were created on purpose. God has a plan for our lives. His will includes the fulfillment of our purpose.

This nutrient is intended to establish confidence and meaning found in our creation. It will also provide an appreciation for and understanding of the sovereignty of God's will.

God Has a Plan

Foundational Scripture
Jeremiah 1:4-5. Then the word of the

Lord came to me, saying: [5] "Before
I formed you in the womb, I knew
you; Before you were born,
I sanctified you;
I ordained you a prophet to the
nations."

In Jeremiah 29:11 God states, "For I know the plans I have for you. Plans for good and not for evil to give you a future and a hope."

God created us for a purpose. He does not waste anything or anyone. There was something missing in the world, there was a problem that needed to be solved; and God hand-crafted you with all the gifts and talents necessary to serve that purpose. He tells Jeremiah that He knew him before he was formed in his mother's womb. God already had a plan for Jeremiah's life. In Jeremiah 29:11 God details the type of plan that He crafts for us. God's plan is for good and not for evil. His plan is to give us a future and hope. God's purpose for our life is best, because His purpose is the path which perfectly aligns to who we are.

The Will of God

It is important for us to identify God's will for our lives. We must live our lives in alignment with His will. We must strive to determine what God seeks to do through our lives. We do not have to go far to find the answers to these questions; for God's purpose lies within us. John 14:20 states, "But the Counselor, the Holy Spirit, whom the Father will send in my name, will teach you all things and will remind you of everything I have said to you." Therefore, we do not have to rely on other people to tell us God's will for our lives. God will tell us and show us through the Holy Spirit within us. If, by chance, God sends someone to speak to us clarifying God's will for our life, the Holy Spirit will agree. God will provide the confirmation. There are many false prophets in the world, who will attempt to lead you down the wrong path. Therefore, we must always stay in alignment with the word of God; so that we will not be led astray. God's will always align to His word.

We can pray to God and ask Him to reveal His will. James 4:2 states, "You do not have, because you do not ask God." When we take the time to reflect on our journey, we can see God's hand. God uses everything on our journey, every mountaintop and every valley has a purpose. God will use those mountaintops and valleys to prepare us for His purpose and calling for our lives. It is important to pay attention to the lessons and preparation God is providing along the way.

Once we ask God to reveal His will, we cannot doubt God's answer. For the Bible says in James 1:6-7, "When he asks, he must believe and not doubt, because he who doubts is like a wave of the sea, blown and tossed by the wind." God's word is true. He created us and He loves us. He will not lead us down the wrong path. He wants the best for us. Therefore, if God says, "Go," we do not need to question Him. He is sovereign.

The word of God will also be a guide. Psalms 119:105 states, "Your word is a lamp to my feet and a light for my path." We must read and study God's word. Once we know God's word, we can disprove any false word that comes to us. We must ask God for the understanding of His word. If we ask Him, He will reveal and He will provide understanding. He has equipped us with everything we need to be successful in what He has called us to do.

We must then stay the course. Once God reveals His purpose for our life, we will encounter obstacles. We should not waste time working in an area that God has not ordained us to work in for that season. But we must work to do what we are called to do. For it is then, and only then, that we can truly please God. There is a difference between being capable and being called. We are often capable of doing many different things. However, in each season God has called us to a specific role within His plan. We have to seek God's will for the season we are in.

We must also be persistent and determined. In Luke 18:1-8 the determination of a widow is portrayed in this parable. She was determined to receive justice. She did not stop because she was told no. Paul endured much persecution during his walk with Christ. But he did not allow the persecution to take him off his course of fulfilling His purpose. He pressed forward. We must also stand firm and press forward. For we know that God is with us. We have his favor. "If God be for us, who can be against us." Come what may, we have the all-powerful, all knowing, and ever-present God on our side. We have the wonderful, counselor, mighty God, everlasting father, and Prince of Peace on our side. We have the healer, deliverer, way maker, protector, and friend on our side. We have God; therefore, we have the victory!

Even in the times when we do not feel victorious, or when we feel hurt and broken, we still have God. We still have the assurance that He will work all things together for our good. As Paul said, in 2 Corinthians 4:8-9, “We are hard pressed on every side, but not crushed; perplexed, but not in despair; persecuted, but not abandoned; struck down, but not destroyed.”

We must be grounded and rooted in God and in His will. For even a broken tree with strong roots can still survive. Upon our rising in the morning, we must connect to God. Throughout the day, we must connect with God. Before we lay down to sleep, we must connect with God. The prophet Isaiah lets us know that 'He will keep you in perfect peace those whose mind is stayed on Him.' We must focus on Him, who is the author and finisher of our faith. We must focus on Him, who is able to keep us from falling. We must focus on Him who cares for us.

So even in the most difficult times, stay in alignment with God's will and His grace. God's will results in victory. So as the song says, "Let us march on till victory is won."

Increasing Territory

Foundational Scripture

1 Chronicles 4:9-10. Now Jabez was more honorable than his brothers, and his mother called his name Jabez,

saying, "Because I bore him in pain." [10]And Jabez called on the God of Israel saying, "Oh, that You would bless me indeed, and enlarge my territory, that Your hand would be with me, and that You would keep me from evil, that I may not cause pain!" God granted him what he requested.

Although Jabez was more honorable than his brothers, he was named Jabez because his mother bore him in pain. Jabez wanted to transcend the meaning of his name. People often try to label us. People may try to assign limitations to us. But through God, we can be elevated above the limits that were placed by man. We can go beyond the man-made boundaries and ceilings. Jabez asked that his territory be enlarged.

In order for us to have our territory enlarged we must go beyond our comfort zone. Our comfort may be within our current territory. But to be enlarged we must extend boldly into a new space outside that place of comfort. We can enter boldly because it is ours; and God will be with us.

We will transcend any labels or limitations that others try to put on us. Jabez prayed a prayer asking God to bless him and to enlarge his territory. This is a prayer that many of us pray today, God heard the prayer of Jabez and granted him his blessing. Therefore, it is helpful to examine his prayer.

Verse 10 begins by saying, "And Jabez called on the God of Israel..." Jabez had a desire, and he went to God. At times we go to God as our last resort, instead of our first option. We tend to rely on the physical things we can see. But these things do not have the power to give us the desires of our heart. The physical things or people we often rely on are unable to discern the appropriate season for our blessing. It does no good to receive a blessing out of season. God gives us the desires of our heart when we are ready for it. The Bible says in Matthew 6:33, "Seek ye first the kingdom of God and His righteousness and all these things will be added unto you." We must go to God for our needs and desires.

Jabez continues his prayer and states, "Oh that You would bless me indeed and enlarge my territory, that your hand would be with me, and that you would keep me from evil that I may not cause pain!" He makes his request known; and he also made his intentions known. He did not simply ask for what he wanted. The Bible says in James 4:2-3, "You do not have, because you do not ask God, you do not receive, because you ask with wrong motives, that you may spend what you get on your pleasures." Our motives and our intent matters. We have to know why we are asking for our request. We need to identify and understand our motives and intent.

Jabez also asked that God would be with him. He realized that an increase in territory meant an increase in responsibility. He wanted to use his responsibility for God's glory. He did not want to gain in order to cause envy or jealousy among others. He specifically states that he does not want to cause pain. Once his territory is enlarged, Jabez can then access more people and bring them to Christ.

This great responsibility will require many attributes that require development and testing. An increase in responsibility requires all of the fruits of the spirit found in Galatians 5:22-23. "But the fruit of the Spirit is love, joy, peace, longsuffering, kindness, goodness, faithfulness, gentleness, and self-control. Against such there is no law." These fruits or attributes are available to all who are willing to work for them.

The work to gain these attributes comes in the testing period. It is easy to love someone who loves you. But are we able to love those who hate us, as we are commissioned by Jesus in Matthew 5:44? It is easy to have joy when things are going well. But can we have joy in times of sorrow? In order to truly obtain these attributes, they must be tested. Before God enlarges our territory, He will ensure that we will be able to handle the increase. The Bible says in Matthew 25:21, "Well done, good and faithful servant; you were faithful over a few
things, I will make you ruler over many things."

After hearing his prayer and examining his heart, God saw fit to grant Jabez this blessing. We must make sure that our requests are aligned with the will of God. We must also inspect our intentions. Then we must trust God and His timing. We cannot rush God. God knows us. He knows our hearts; He knows our purpose. He does not desire to grant us something that will destroy us. We must trust His unlimited knowledge; and understand that since He created us, He knows what is best for us. Therefore, while we are awaiting our season of increase, we need to develop our fruit. We should welcome situations that test our patience, try our love, or stretch our self-control. For we are not alone. God is with us. And when the season is right, He will bless us with the increase.

Seasons

Our discernment of seasons is an important component to our understanding of our purpose and God's will. In every season you will experience, God has something for you to gain within that season. Therefore, whatever season you are in, it is your time, and it is your season. You may have been toiling and struggling. You may have been wrestling and hurting. As Donnie McClurkin said in his song "Stand", "You've prayed, and you've cried. And you've prayed and you've cried." But as David says in Psalm 126, "Those who sow in tears, shall reap in joy." You can declare that it is your time. It is your season. 2 Corinthians 6:2 says, "Behold now is the accepted time; behold now is the day of salvation." God says in Isaiah 43, "Behold I will do a new thing and it shall now spring forth." It is a new season.

Ecclesiastes 3 states "to everything there is a season and time for every purpose under heaven." There is a purpose for every season. There is a purpose for your mountaintops and there is purpose of the pain felt in the valley. God is omnipresent. He is present in every season. He is present in the good times. He is present in the hard times. He is present on the mountaintop and present in the valley. The season may change. Relationships may change. Circumstances may change. But our God is the same. God says in Malachi 3, "I am the Lord. I do not change." David said, "God is our refuge and strength a very present help in the time of trouble." He is there.

We have to recognize the season we are in and optimize the season. Our focus needs to be on fulfilling the purpose of your current season. The story of Joseph begins in Genesis 37. Joseph had a life of many seasons. He had a season of favor, a season of dreams, a season of attacks, a season of bondage, and a season of favor while in bondage. That is only part of the story. Joseph was the twelfth son of Jacob. He was born in Jacob's old age. Jacob made it clear that Joseph was his favorite. During the season of favor, he received special gifts, treatment, and training.

However, if not handled carefully and mindfully, favor can bring about jealousy from others. Joseph's mismanagement of favor led to a season of attacks for Joseph. Jealousy got the best of his brothers and they conspired to kill him. His brother Reuben spoke up and said "let us not kill him. Let's just throw him into this pit." In Genesis 37:20, the brothers said, "we shall see what will become of his dreams."

They did not realize the dreams Joseph spoke of were not his dreams; they were the visions of God's plan. No matter how evil the brothers were, no matter how deep the pit Joseph was in, God's plan would prevail. In due season, God was going to turn it around.

The brothers stripped him of his coat of many colors and threw him into the pit. Judah then spoke to his brothers and said, "Why don't we sell him into slavery." The other brothers agreed. They sold Joseph into slavery.

While in bondage, Joseph's gifts made room for him. He was granted the opportunity to use his gift of interpreting dreams. Pharoah had a few dreams that troubled him. Joseph used his God-given gifts to interpret the dreams.

The dreams indicated there would be seven years of plenty, followed by seven years of famine. This interpretation allowed Joseph to provide the appropriate guidance. They should save during the season of plenty so they will be sustained during the season of famine. The time of the famine came; and the famine was all over the face of the Earth. The Bible says all countries came to

Joseph in Egypt to buy grain. Joseph's brothers also came to buy grain; and this fulfilled God's plan.
There was a purpose in the season of plenty and there was purpose in the season of famine. During the years of plenty, they had to prepare for the season of famine to come. In our season of plenty, we cannot forget to prepare. Whether it is a season of plenty in our resources, energy, or time; we must prepare. We must develop the fruits of the spirit (Galatians 5:22-23) and polish the full armor of God (Ephesians 6:10-18) to prepare for the seasons of storms.

Today we categorize storms based on their strength and intensity. Regardless of how strong and how intense the storm may be, God can step into the midst of your storm and say, "Peace be still". Even if the storm does not cease when you want it to cease, God can and will give you the grace and favor to see you through it.

In the seasons of storm, we have to remember, as Paul said in Romans 8, "And we know that in all things work together for good to those who love God, to those who are the called according to His purpose." The Bible also says in Ecclesiastes 3 that God "has made everything beautiful in its time."

Even in the season of famine, God enabled Joseph to have something to give. Do not allow your season to consume you. To keep it from consuming you, keep your focus on Christ.

In Romans 12, Paul says "Do not be conformed to this world but be ye transformed by the renewing of your mind." Do not conform to your season. Do not focus on your sickness; focus on your healer. Do not focus on the limitations; focus on the way maker. For we are more than conquerors through Him who loves us. It is through Him that we conquer. We must be able to focus on Him regardless of what season we may be in. If we do, then God will make all things beautiful in its time. Whether you are in a season of plenty or a season of famine, it is your time and your season. God is able to teach you, bless you, comfort you, prepare you, and guide you in every season. Throughout the changing seasons, hold to God's unchanging hands.

There's a story that I was told when I was younger that relates to changing seasons. There was a man who had four sons. He wanted to teach his sons a lesson. He sent them each on a quest, to go and observe at a pear tree that was in a park quite a distance away. The first son went in the winter, the second in the spring, the third in summer, and the youngest son embarked on the quest in the fall. When they had all gone on their quest and returned, the father called his sons together to describe what they had seen. Then they could determine what to do about the tree.

The first son that went out in the winter said the tree was ugly, dry, bent, and twisted. He thought it was worthless. His recommendation was that they needed to tear that tree down. The second son that went out in the spring said “no, the tree was covered with green buds, and it is full of promise. We just need to give it more time. The third son who observed the tree in the summer disagreed with the two reports from his bothers. He said the tree was full of blossoms that smelled really sweet and looked beautiful. It was nice to look at and should stay just the way it is. The last son that went in the fall disagreed with all of his brothers. He reported that the tree was ripe and drooping with fruit, full of life and fulfilment.

The man then explained to his sons that they were all right, because they had each seen only one season in this tree's life. The lesson in this story is that you cannot judge a tree, or a person, including yourself, by one season.

If you give up when it is winter, you will miss the promise of your spring, the beauty of your summer, and the fulfilment of your fall. Do not judge any life by one difficult and challenging season. Do not let the pain of one season destroy the joy and purpose of all the those to come. One season will not diminish your purpose. If you continue to learn, grow, and develop the season will change.

Witnessing is part of our purpose

Once we become Christians, we are commissioned to share the gospel of Jesus Christ with others. The Bible says in Matthew 28:19, "Go therefore, and make disciples of all the nations, baptizing them in the name of the father, and of the Son, and of the Holy Spirit, teaching them to observe all things that I have commanded you; and lo, I am with you always even until the end of the age. Amen." This may seem like an enormous task to accomplish; but actually, it is not. Once we fully give Jesus control over our lives, sharing about Him is easy. He is too good to keep to ourselves. David said in Psalms 23:5, "My cup runs over." His power is too awesome; it explodes. His grace is too wonderful; it overflows. His love is too amazing; it floods our hearts. We cannot keep him to ourselves.

There are many opportunities to share the beauty of salvation with others. When Jesus set the demon-possessed man free, the delivered man wanted to stay with Jesus. However, Jesus tells him in Mark 5:19, "Go home to your friends, and tell them what great things the Lord has done for you, and how He has had compassion on you." However, when we are not focused on Jesus, we allow these opportunities to pass by us.

When we may be sent into uncomfortable places to share the gospel, the Holy Spirit will guide us. In Acts 8:26-40, Philip was sent to minister to an Ethiopian. Philip had to follow the specific instructions of the Lord. If we follow the instructions of God, we will not fail. We may not be the ones to ultimately bring the person to salvation through Christ. God may want us to simply plant a seed. Someone else may be called to water the seed; and someone else may be called to nurture it until it grows. We must stay in the will of God and do our part.

Our lives should be a consistent witness to the grace and power of God. Others are watching what we say, what we do, and how we live. In Acts 16, when Paul and Silas were in prison, in the midst of their torture and bondage, verse 25 says that Paul and Silas were praying and singing hymns to God. Verse 25 also says that the other prisoners were listening. When the foundations of the prison were shaken it was not only Paul and Silas' chains that were loosened. All the prison doors were opened, and everyone's chains came loose. What Paul and Silas chose to do in the midnight hour when things were at their darkest, freed them and everyone that was present.

Let your life be like the burning bush Moses saw in Exodus 3. Let God speak through your life. In Exodus 3, Moses saw a bush that was engulfed in flames; but it was not burning up. It was out of that bush that God spoke to Moses. There are times in life where we are in the midst of the fires and trials of this world. But if we do not allow the fires to overtake us. If we maintain our peace, love, and joy in Christ. Then through our trials, God will speak to others. When others see you, they should not see your situation; they should see your savior and your faith in Him.

We never know who may be watching our lives. However, we know there is one who sees it all. The Bible says, "The eyes of the Lord are in everything, beholding the evil and the good." Therefore, we must always be prepared to live a life that is a witness of the grace and goodness of God.

There is not a set script on how to witness to someone. In order to be an effective witness, we must follow the direction of the Holy Spirit. For God knows the heart of every man. He knows what words need to be heard and what actions need to be seen. Therefore, we must allow Him to take control. Before ever approaching anyone, we must pray to God asking Him to speak for us and asking for His guidance. For without His guidance, we will accomplish nothing. Without His words, our speech will be in vain. We may say all the right things; but without the spirit of God behind it, it will mean nothing. God says, "If I be lifted up, I will draw all men unto me." We cannot draw anyone; He is the one that will draw them to Himself.

Since Jesus paid the price of salvation by dying on the cross. The road to salvation has been made easy for us. All we must do is confess our sins; believe that Jesus died on the cross for our sins and that He rose with all power. And finally, we must invite him to come into and lead our lives.

Paul is a great example and witness of God's grace and power. Paul's name was once Saul. He was a sinner, who persecuted Christians. However, in Acts 9 on the road of Damascus, Saul's life changed forever. His name was changed to Paul; and he grew into a mighty warrior for Christ. We must get to the point in our walk with Christ that we can proclaim, as Paul did in Romans 1:16, "For I am not ashamed of the gospel of Jesus Christ, for it is the power of God to salvation for everyone who believes."

The first people chosen to share the news about Jesus' resurrection were Mary Magdalene, Joanna, Mary the mother of James, and the other women with them (Luke 24:9-10; Matthew 28:10). God will empower us to do that which He calls us to do. Jesus died for us. All He asks is that we believe in Him, allow Him to help us through life, and share Him with others. Therefore, when God needs a work completed, let us be strong enough to say, "Here am I, Lord, send me!"

You must be willing to allow your cup to run over. You should share His goodness; and represent Jesus in all you do. You should let the world see that you are who you are in Christ. You must be consistent in your walk on the path of spiritual growth. You can walk with the assurance that your God is all-powerful. You can know and claim the promises of God. Let your life be a witness; and walk in VICTORY!

Nutrient 7 –Praise and Worship

The Intention of This Nutrient: Praise brings perspective. Perspective is defined as the chosen point of view that drives someone's understanding. When we look at our lives, we can choose a perspective that highlights all the wrong and pain in our past, or all the problems in our present. But another perspective is to praise God for allowing us to overcome and still be standing. We can praise God for enabling us to create a future that is different than our past.

Paul tells us in Philippians 4 that we are to acknowledge God in all things. When we acknowledge His presence, power, and promise we will see a new perspective. It is impossible to complain and praise God at the same time. When complaints go up, your mentality creates a block to the blessings you could have. On the other hand, it is true that when praises go up, blessings come down. When you worship God for who He is and praise God for what He has already done, you will adopt a spirit of expectation. You will strengthen your faith. You will choose the perspective of praise.

There are images that contain optical illusions, such as the one below.

Multiple people can look at this same image but what they see may be different. Someone may see an older woman, and someone else may see the younger woman in the image. As Henry David Thoreau once said, "It's not what you look at that matters, it's what you see."

Sometimes, it takes someone else to point out the other image within the same picture. In life it may take other people to help you put things into proper perspective. It may take someone else to point out blessings we may overlook. To wake up in the morning is a blessing. To have food to eat is a blessing. To have a roof over our head is a blessing. To have a purpose for our lives is a blessing. God is truly good. He is better than good. He is worthy to be praised!

As all other nutrients are consumed, this critical nutrient automatically appears. Once you truly understand the majestic identity that our God has, and the magnitude of His power, your heart will long to worship Him. Whenever you think of His goodness that He demonstrates through the promises, favor, mercy, and grace He gives us, you will want to praise Him. As you unpack your own journey and see all that God has put in you to enable you to come through your journey, and as you understand His will for your life; you will praise Him for His intentionality. Let everything that has breath praise the Lord!

True worship requires that we worship Him in spirit and in truth. John 4 states, "God is spirit, and those who worship Him must worship Him in spirit and in truth." Our focus must be in the right place. Our focus must be on Him.

Matthew, Mark, Luke, and John document the story of Jesus being anointed with perfume from an alabaster box. Jesus was in Bethany and was invited to a dinner at the house of a Pharisee named Simon. Simon was once stricken with leprosy. While at his home, Lazarus whom Jesus had recently raised from the dead days earlier was there with his sisters Mary and Martha. The disciples were also present. Martha was serving the guests. Mary came with an alabaster box full of a perfumed oil, called spikenard. The perfumed oil cost the equivalent of one year's salary. Mary poured the oil on Jesus' head and his feet. She was weeping and her tears fell on Jesus, and she wiped his feet with her hair. There were several people in the same place at the same event, but their focus was not on Jesus.

Luke tells us that when Simon the leper who invited Jesus, saw Mary anointing him he said to himself that if Jesus was really a prophet, he would know who is touching him and what kind of woman she is. She is a sinner.
Although Simon was speaking to himself, Jesus responded with a parable. Two men owed a lender money. One owed the lender 500 denarii and the other owed 50 denarii. Neither had the money to pay the

debt. The lender forgave the debt of both men. Jesus asked Simon which man loved the lender more? Simon answered, “the one with the larger debt forgiven.”

Jesus then made it plain. Simon was focused on Mary’s sin as he felt her sin was much greater than his own. Jesus said to Simon, “You invited me into your home. But you did not give me water for my feet. You did not give me a greeting of a kiss. You did not anoint my head with oil. But this woman did all these things.” Simon had invited Jesus into his home. But then forgot about Him. Simon was focused on others’ sins and lost sight of Jesus. We have to be careful to keep Jesus as the focus. We invite Jesus into our hearts, into our home, and into our church. But we cannot get distracted. Jesus is not just an invited guest. He is the focus; He is the center.

Additionally, in this story, Martha was not focused on Jesus. John tells us that Martha was busy serving. Working for Jesus is important. But we must not forget to keep Him as the focus, even in our work and service.

Another perspective was that of Judas. Judas was also not focused on Jesus. He felt Mary's worship was too costly. He felt it was wasteful. He felt her time and money would be better spent somewhere else. Judas responds to Mary's worship by saying, "why waste this oil? This oil is worth one year's salary. It could have been sold and given to the poor."

John reveals Judas' true intent because things are not always what they seem. On the surface this seems right. Giving the money to the poor is a noble action to take. However, John tells us that Judas did not say this out of concern for the poor. But Judas was the treasurer; and he was also a thief. He would take money from the treasury. Judas was focused on what he could get, and how he could profit from this event. But Jesus said in Mark 8 for "what will it profit a man the gain the whole world and lose his soul."

Then there was the perspective of Mary. To fully understand Mary's focus, we have to go back a chapter. In John 11, Mary's brother Lazarus had died. Upon arriving at the tomb, Jesus told the people there to roll the stone away. Lazarus was buried in a tomb whose entrance was sealed with a stone. Martha then raised her voice and said "Lord, by this time there is a stench, for he's been dead four days." Jesus said to her "Did I not tell you if you would believe you would see the glory of God?" They rolled the stone away and Jesus cried out to Lazarus saying "Lazarus, come forth!". And Lazarus came out of the tomb.

When Jesus first asked them to roll the stone away, Martha was worried about the smell and didn't want the stone rolled away. At times we hide behind stones because we listen to other's voices, and sometimes our own voice, that says "no one wants to smell the stench of your sin. No one wants to hear your story or see your pain." So, we then hide. We hide behind substances, bad relationships, behind masks, and performances. But we have to roll the stone away and say "Lord here I am. I have removed all the layers and here I stand in my truth, in my brokenness, and in my pain. I need your resurrection power." Mary saw what happens when you remove the stones. When you remove the stones, and expose your authentic stench, when you expose the state you are in; Jesus will activate his resurrection power.

Mary made her way to Jesus, carrying this jar of oil which cost so much; but

Jesus deserved it all. Mary did not call for everyone's attention. She did not pass around the price tag for her oil. She was not focused on the others in the room. She was only focused on Jesus, the one who heals, the one who saves, the one who delivers. Though they talked about her, she pressed on and praised Him. They told her that her praise was too costly, she pressed on anyway and praised Him. She poured out all she had for Jesus. The fragrance of her worship filled the room.

We have to do as Mary did. We have to focus on Jesus. He deserves our worship; and He deserves our praise. With this in mind, I will declare, Lord, I am rolling back the stones that I have been hiding behind. I am giving it all to you - everything I have, everything I am. I am going to keep pouring out to you oh God until the fragrance of worship fills this place where I am currently standing.

I remember what it felt like to experience God's resurrection power. Through his resurrection power, God is able to raise, call forth, and to cause us to breathe again. The grip of the struggle of life can wrap around you so tightly, you can feel as if you cannot breathe. There are some seasons you my face where you can experience struggle with no relief. You may be enduring daily trauma; and you can feel as if you are drowning in the tears of heartache and pain. But at my lowest and darkest moment, Jesus saved me. He delivered me and resurrected my hopes and my dreams.

People may not understand your praise. Sometimes they do not understand my praise. For those that do not understand, I tell them, "You may see that I am saved, but you do not know what God saved me from. You may see that I have been delivered but you do not know what he has delivered me out of. You do not know my valleys like I know my valleys. You do not know how much grace it took to save me. You do not know how much of his blood had to flow in order to reach me in the valley I was in.

So, I choose to do as David did; and regardless of how I feel, I will command myself to praise Him. I will bless the Lord at all times; His praise shall continually be in my mouth. I will bless the Lord Oh my soul and all that is within me. I will praise His holy name.

I do not praise God based on how I feel. I praise God based on what I know. And I know that He is faithful. I know that He is merciful. When I think of the goodness of Jesus, I am reminded that He is a way maker. When I think of the goodness of Jesus, I am reminded that He is a promise keeper. And it is those things, it is that knowledge, it is that truth, that causes my soul to cry out hallelujah!

Worship God for who He is. Praise Him for all that He has done through His mighty power. Praise Him for His faithfulness in keeping His promises. Praise Him for His mercy and grace. Praise Him for His intentionality in creating us for a purpose. Let everything that has breath praise the Lord!

Hallelujah! Thank you, Jesus! To God be the glory!

References

1. **Identity** – 1 John 5:7, John 1:1, John 1:14, Exodus 3:1-14, Isaiah 9:2-6, Isaiah 60:1-3, John 1:4-5, 2 Chronicles 20, Psalms 91:14-15, Matthew 9:27-31, Philippians 2:10, Psalms 139:14, Matthew 11:28, Psalms 24:8, Genesis 17:1, Psalms 90:2, Hebrews 13:8, John 14:27, Philippians 4:7, Mark 4:39, Matthew 7, John 10:27, Matthew 16:13-19, Romans 10, Acts 3:1-10, Acts 4:1-12, Mark 10: 46-52, 1 Peter 2:9, Ephesian 1:11, Jeremiah 29:11, Romans 12:6, Mark 5:35-43

2. **Power** – Matthew 11, Genesis 1, Genesis 2:18, Zechariah 4:6, Mark 4:35-41, Matthew 14:13-21, 1 Kings 17:8-16, Mark 5:21-43, John 5:1-9, Matthew 8:1-13, Daniel 3:15-30, Daniel 6, Mark 4:25-41, Psalms119:105, Exodus 14:5-21, Joshua 3, Matthew 17, Genesis 6:13-22, Provers 3, John 11:38-44, Matthew 27: 11-66, Acts 2:22-25, John 16:33, Ephesians 6, Psalms 23, Genesis 6-8, Exodus 3-14, Daniel 3, Daniel 6, Mark 5, James 3

Hoffman, Elisha. "I must tell Jesus." The New National Baptist Hymnal 21st Century Edition, 2001, p.340.

Holm, D. (1983). Rise Again. [Recorded by D. Holm & Praise]. On *Live/ Rise Again* [Vinyl]. Greentree Records.

3. **Promises** - Psalm 23, Isaiah 55:11, Malachi 3:10-12, Genesis 25:30-33, Genesis 27:18-30, Genesis 28:11-22, Genesis 30:29-43, Exodus 12:12-13, Ephesians 6:1-3, Deuteronomy 28:1-68, Jeremiah 1:4-5, Matthew 5:3-12, Mark 5, 2 Corinthians 12, Luke 15, John 14, Numbers 12, Daniel 6, 2 Chronicles 7:14, Matthew 7:7, Romans 8:28, Psalms 17:3, Daniel 3, Matthew 21, Joshua 24, Acts 16,

A Testament of Hope: The Essential Writings and Speeches of Martin Luther King, Jr., ed. by James M. Washington, Harper San Francisco (1986)

4. **Mercy** -Psalms 51, Romans 3:23, Romans 6:23, Isaiah 43:25, Psalms 32, 1 Peter 1:8, 2 Chronicles 7, 2 Chronicles 6, Romans 8, John 10, Romans 12, Matthew 6, Philippians 3, Luke 13:10-13, John 16:33, 1 Peter 4, John 11, Psalms 23, Matthew 26, 2 Corinthians 4, Matthew 5, Luke 23:34, Matthew 27, John 8:1-11, Exodus 15:26, John 3:16, 1 Corinthians 1:18, Isaiah 59:2, Ephesians

2:12, 1 Peter 5:8, Proverbs 13:21-22, Haggai 1:6, Psalms 30:5, Isaiah 53:5-6, John 1:12, Revelations 3:20

Rowe, James. "Love lifted me." The New National Baptist Hymnal 21st Century Edition, 2001, p.385.

Spafford, Horatio. "It is well with my soul." The New National Baptist Hymnal 21st Century Edition, 2001, p.255.

Wesley, Charles. "Father, I stretch my hands to thee." The New National Baptist Hymnal 21st Century Edition, 2001, p.42.

5. **Grace** – John 16:33, 1 Corinthians 15:9-10, 2 Corinthians 12:7-10, 2 Corinthians 12:8, Ephesians 2:8, Romans 8:18, Mark 4, 1 Peter 5, Matthew 8, John 3:16, John 10:10

Crouch, Andrae. "The blood will never lose its power." The New National Baptist Hymnal 21st Century Edition, 2001, p.146.

Lowry, Robert. “Nothing but the blood.” The New National Baptist Hymnal 21st Century Edition, 2001, p.141.

6. **Purpose** - Jeremiah 1:4-5, Jeremiah 29:11, John 14:20, James 4:2, James 1:6-7, Psalms 119:105, Luke 18:1-8, 2 Corinthians 4:8-9, 1 Chronicles 4:9-10, James 4:2-3, Galatians 5:22-23, Matthew 5:44, Matthew 25:21, 2 Corinthians 6:2, Isaiah 43, Ecclesiastes 3, Malachi 3, Genesis 37, Romans 8, Romans 12, Matthew 28:19, Psalms 23, Mark 5:19, Acts 8:26-40, Acts 16, Exodus 3, Acts 9, Romans 1:16, Luke 24:9-10, Matthew 28:10

Allers, R., & Minkoff, R. (1994). *The Lion King*. Buena Vista Pictures.

McClurkin, D (1996). Stand [Recorded by Donnie McClurkin]. On *Donnie McClurkin.* Sony/ATV Music Publishing LLC, Warner Alliance.

7. **Praise and Worship** – Philippians 4, John 4, Mark 8, John 11

"Types of Optical Illusions." *Clear Eyes*, Prestige Consumer Healthcare Inc, 2022, https://www.cleareyes.com/eye-care-blog/201610/types-optical-illusions.